Humanitarian Intervention

The Japan Center for International Exchange wishes to thank

Asia Pacific Agenda Project

HUMANITARIAN
INTERVENTION
The Evolving Asian Debate

edited by
Watanabe Kōji

JCIE

Tokyo • Japan Center for International Exchange • *New York*

The surnames of the authors and other persons mentioned in this book
are positioned according to country practice.

Copyediting by Lidia Rényi and Pamela J. Noda.
Cover and typographic design by Becky Davis, EDS Inc., Editorial & Design
Services. Typesetting and production by EDS Inc.
Cover photograph © Corbis Digital Stock

Printed in Japan.
ISBN 4-88907-066-4

Distributed outside Japan by Brookings Institution Press (1775 Massachusetts
Avenue, N.W., Washington, D.C. 20036-2188 U.S.A.) and Kinokuniya
Company Ltd. (5-38-1 Sakuragaoka, Setagaya-ku, Tokyo 156-8691 Japan).

Japan Center for International Exchange
9-17 Minami Azabu 4-chome, Minato-ku, Tokyo 106-0047 Japan
URL: http://www.jcie.or.jp

Japan Center for International Exchange, Inc. (JCIE/USA)
274 Madison Avenue, Suite 1102, New York, N.Y. 10016 U.S.A.
URL: http://www.jcie.org

Contents

Foreword

WITH the intervention in Kosovo by the North Atlantic Treaty Organization in 1999 and the situation in East Timor gradually beginning to pose serious questions to the international community, it seemed extremely important for a consortium of policy research institutions such as the Asia Pacific Agenda Project (APAP) to examine the nature and legitimacy of forceful interventions among the international community. Acting upon this conviction, the APAP steering committee in the fall of 2000 requested Ambassador Watanabe Kōji to direct a multilateral research project on the theme of force, intervention, and sovereignty in the Asian theatre. Following the APAP tradition of joint research projects, a study group was formed under the guidance of Ambassador Watanabe by recruiting younger scholars from China, India, Japan, South Korea, and the Association of Southeast Asian Nations (ASEAN) as paper writers.

Whether states have the right to intervene forcefully in the sovereign affairs of others when their own interests are considered threatened or their values affronted has always been a contentious issue in international relations. Current trends suggest that this question will only grow more acute in the years ahead. Before the terrorist attacks of September 11, 2001, in the United States, most Asian countries were reluctant to condone forceful intervention, especially for humanitarian reasons. Having experienced a chain of events—the East Asian financial crisis, the so-called haze problem emanating from Indonesia, the Australian-led intervention for peace enforcement missions, threats from post–9-11 international terrorism, and war in Iraq—however, many Asians are beginning to rethink whether there are limits to the general principle of nonintervention. A debate is beginning on the value and meaning of nonintervention in a region that is becoming increasingly interdependent. The mostly undisclosed discussions on Myanmar before and during the ASEAN Bali Summit in October 2003 is only the most recent example of this new attitude on the part of ASEAN countries, which have long been known for their strictly nonintervention policy. With the likelihood that future crises both outside and inside the region will arise to challenge prevalent attitudes and policy, this debate is likely to intensify, with significant implications for Asia's political development.

Drafts of the chapters herein were presented as papers and discussed at the Global ThinkNet (GTN) conference that took place in Tokyo in November 2001. Comments and suggestions offered during the conference were incorporated by the authors as they finalized their respective papers. Because the papers were completed before the dust of 9-11 had subsided, some analyses and conclusions presented in this volume may be slightly outdated. It has taken us much longer to complete the processes necessary to publish the book than we expected. Nevertheless, I firmly believe that the discussions and examinations presented here constitute significant contributions to the continuous global discussion on the theme of forceful intervention and its relation to the notion of sovereignty.

I wish to take this opportunity to express our deepest and sincere gratitude to Ambassador Watanabe and all the authors who took up this challenging task and to congratulate them for having successfully completed the task. I also wish to thank various funding organizations, most notably the Japanese government, whose generous grant to APAP made it possible to conduct this project.

Tadashi Yamamoto
President
Japan Center for International Exchange
Secretariat
Asia Pacific Agenda Project

Humanitarian Intervention

1. The Debate on Humanitarian Intervention

Watanabe Kōji

WHEN a massive and systematic violation of basic human rights is committed by the authorities of one state, can other states intervene forcefully to halt the violation? Since the North Atlantic Treaty Organisation's (NATO's) military intervention in Kosovo in 1999, the issue of what is now commonly called humanitarian intervention has become one of the most contentious subjects in managing contemporary international relations. Conspicuous in the argument on Kosovo has been the fact that most Asian countries were opposed to, or reluctant to endorse, the use of force by NATO against the Federal Republic of Yugoslavia.

The Force, Intervention, and Sovereignty Project grew out of the recognition that there was a distinct need to clarify the positions of Asian countries to the extent possible, so that any future dispute between them and members of the Atlantic alliance on the matter of international intervention—albeit defined as humanitarian—would not develop into a situation affecting the peaceful global environment. The project was designed to promote a comparative analysis of the views held on intervention by China, India, Japan, South Korea, and member states of the Association of Southeast Asian Nations (ASEAN). In the following pages, the project members have identified areas of consensus and divergence and set forth practical policy recommendations.

ASIAN VIEWS

In Asia, the subject of both international and humanitarian intervention has elicited attitudes ranging from negative to ambivalent, reflecting interrelated factors shared to varying degrees, including historical experience, developing-country status, small- and/or weak-state status, problems with the West, and the concept of the "Asian way." Prior to World War II, most Asian countries were colonized or subjected to foreign domination, which historical experience has left them sensitive to foreign intervention and jealous guardians of their sovereignty.

Inasmuch as the West is considered the advocate of democracy, human rights, and the rule of law—so-called Western values—some Asian countries reject intervention by Western countries as an imposition of Western values on Asians, or more Western dominance. While debate continues on the question of whether a cohesive set of Asian values does, in fact, exist, there is certainly a vague pattern of behavior that is recognized by many as the Asian way. Often cited as a typical instance is the ASEAN policy of nonintervention.

Considering that ASEAN is composed of a diverse set of nations in terms of size, political system, stage of economic development, and religious faith, one is inclined to appreciate and value the pragmatism of the policy. Moreover, the fact that these developing countries have a common history of having been dominated by the West, are relatively weak states, and have diverse identities while at the same time being distinct from the West makes them skeptical of the notion of humanitarian intervention in general.

China

On the matter of international intervention, Jia Qingguo explains in chapter 2 that China's posture is a reflection of "the nature of the existing international system; China's experience with the outside world in modern times; its international status; and its domestic politics." Beijing has found itself best able to defend its interests in international relations by adhering to the code of national sovereignty, in the recognition that states will inevitably assert these rights in their own separate ways. While this view has drawn ridicule from detractors at home and abroad, Jia appeals for our understanding of it and the historical constraints on which it is based.

Beijing has opposed international intervention in its internal affairs since 1949, the birth of the People's Republic of China, in the belief that the sovereignty of nation-states and the right of developing countries to be free from foreign intervention in their internal affairs should be respected by the international community, according to the precepts of international law and standards of morality. While it is the duty of each country to protect human rights within its borders, no country has the right to "assume moral superiority and impose its preferences on others," each country having the right to determine how it shall protect human rights "in light of its economic, social, political, and cultural priorities." Thus, China was one of those countries most critical of NATO's intervention in Kosovo, denouncing the act as a flagrant violation of international law because it did not have the approval of the UN Security Council.

In sum, Jia throws down the gauntlet: China's position is consistent with international law; international intervention has no legitimate basis and violates the Charter of the United Nations; such intercession is mostly conducted to further the interests of the intervening, rather than the target state; and the net result is that existing problems are usually exacerbated in terms of the proclaimed objectives. Historically, intervention in the internal affairs of developing countries has been either the handiwork of developed countries or at their instigation. Still in the process of nation-state building, developing Asian countries are socially and politically fragile, and some are experiencing ethnic and religious minority problems.

In the sense that weak states do not intervene forcefully in the affairs of powerful states, most countries in Asia consider themselves in a weaker position relative to the developed countries, making them more concerned about being targeted for intervention than about intervening. Although the stronger of the developing countries may be tempted to intervene in the affairs of weaker states—China and India may harbor that temptation—their position relative to the West is for the most part inferior in the power equation. The image of the West as more powerful is particularly potent when the West is associated, as is generally the case, with the United States, the world's sole superpower.

Japan

Japan, although never colonized, was a colonial power that committed acts of aggression against Asian states. This historical legacy has, as Murata Kōji relates in chapter 3, left Japan averse to the notion of the use of force and, by extension, intervention.

As stipulated by its 1947 Constitution, Japan has renounced the use of force, and is sensitive to the charge of intervention into the domestic affairs of other states. Thus, the official Japanese position on the NATO military intervention in Kosovo was that of understanding, not outright endorsement or approval. Japan did not endorse NATO's action because of the perceived legal difficulties surrounding justification of the action under established international law. The Kosovo case was markedly different from the case of the Gulf War in 1990, when Japan approved and supported the military action by the multilateral force against Iraq, since the United Nations Security Council had authorized the multilateral force to exercise the right of collective defense of the sovereign state of Kuwait.

The nub of the issue appears to revolve around whether the principles of state sovereignty are seen to be violated when international intervention seeks to halt the actions of a government involved in infringing human rights or to intercede, for humanitarian reasons, in a civil war. The conditions and means of intervention are key. Once again we are reminded that in such theaters of conflict as Kosovo and Afghanistan, the use of the term humanitarian may be difficult for some to justify.

Muddying the waters of Japan's official response both to incidents of international intervention and the call for Tokyo to assist, as a willing partner, in such intervention, is the government's current interpretation of its constitution, which is open to various interpretations with regard to the role of the Self-Defense Forces (SDF) and the country's right to self-defense. Because the government believed that the country has the right to collective self-defense, but cannot exercise it, it was not until the early 1990s that it made any effort to participate in UN-sponsored peacekeeping operations (PKOs). In 2002, as a result of the gradual change in the country's perceptions of security and under the revised PKO Law, 690 SDF personnel were dispatched to East Timor, marking a sea change in the country's stance on intervention.

South Korea

In chapter 4, Kim Sung-han reminds us that the major threats to human rights have, during the post–cold war era, come from quasi and failed states in which there has been civil strife and complex emergencies. Even though at such times intervention has been carried out in a bid to limit human suffering and death, it should be borne in mind that intervention, involving the use of force by one state within the borders of another without the latter's concurrence, violates the sovereignty of the state in which the intervention occurs and, without the authorization of the UN Security Council, is illegal unless justified as self-defense.

Over the centuries, emphasis has moved from religious toleration to minority rights, human rights and, more recently, to human security, which includes "security against economic privation, an acceptable quality of life, and a guarantee of fundamental human rights," all of which aspects are recognized as basic if there is to be peace and stability. Kim underlines the paradox that, while nonintervention is considered vital to the functioning of international society, states have, nevertheless, intervened because of the oligarchic nature of international relations that was strengthened at the end of the cold war and left both the United States as the sole superpower, and military force the linchpin of its foreign policy. Since the end of the cold war, the United States has, thus, justified humanitarian military intervention as a way of promoting peace.

And so it was that, in March 1999, NATO used force against Yugoslavia, also on the grounds that to do so was necessary to avert an impending human catastrophe. However, the systemic violations of human rights in Kosovo were not halted by NATO intervention. In stark contrast, however, the intervention in East Timor reaffirmed the long-accepted rules of international intervention, for Indonesia gave its consent, the UN Security Council its authorization, and all the criteria for legitimate humanitarian intervention were met.

Kim also raises the matter of human security, pointing out the importance of controlling knowledge and information. Networking and coalition building could help address human rights abuses, international crime, and human security issues, thereby bolstering democracy.

The Korean position on intervention is somewhat similar to that of Japan, in the sense that South Korea is a member of the Organization of Economic Cooperation and Development (OECD), a grouping of industrial democracies respecting democracy, human rights, and the rule of law. Although South Korea was colonized by Japan, the attitude of its people toward humanitarian intervention is, nevertheless, more positive than in most other Asian countries. Active South Korean participation in the peacekeeping operation in East Timor exemplifies this. At the same time, South Korea has its own problems related to North Korea, concerning which it would seem a case can probably be made for human rights violations.

India

As Jasjit Singh expounds in chapter 5, intervention is carried out by the strong against the weak, and by the developed countries of the West against the developing countries of the South. He also reminds us that "[i]t is important to note that there is as yet no viable alternative to the system of the sovereign state," and that with the world order having become polycentric, the principle of sovereignty should be strengthened. Coping with the problem of human rights violations requires looking into its causes and taking preventive measures, not resorting to military means. "The needs of humanitarian intervention must be met with assistance aimed at building the nation-state, rather than military intervention in its name."

Although support has been forthcoming from developing countries for international intervention by Western countries when carried out under the auspices of the United Nations, problems have arisen in such cases when the United Nations has been marginalized, as happened in Kosovo.

The bitter criticism and strong reservations concerning NATO's action in Kosovo notwithstanding, no country in Asia seems to be categorically rejecting the notion of humanitarian intervention as such.

India militarily intervened in Pakistan in 1970, and China supported anti-government forces in South Africa for many years. While both cases could have been motivated by strategic and political considerations, humanitarian factors were also cited as justification.

ASEAN

ASEAN member countries, comprising mainly small to medium-sized states, have been disquieted and ambivalent about NATO's actions in Kosovo. Since the use of force is strictly limited under international law and the NATO allies failed to seek specific UN authorization, many ASEAN member countries saw the Kosovo situation as a matter of power politics rather than a moral question. As Simon S. C. Tay and Rizal Sukma eloquently discuss in chapter 6, intervention—albeit for humanitarian reasons—has become a significant aspect of the ASEAN notion of state sovereignty as, with globalization and the related trans-formations that have taken place in some ASEAN countries, there has arisen a need for cooperation beyond the interests of states to include broader human concerns.

The authors explore a range of ASEAN views, from the changing context of nonintervention debate in ASEAN states to the fact that member states are becoming increasingly differentiated. Thus, while the ASEAN policy of nonintervention—that benign aloofness and tol-erance that one country maintains vis-à-vis the internal affairs of another—remains firmly in place, efforts in the direction of flexible engagement and acceptance of enhanced interaction are proceeding. For example, the role played by the Philippines and Thailand in East Timor peacekeeping efforts suggests that some ASEAN countries are more positive about humanitarian intervention than others. Bearing this in mind, it may be necessary, the authors suggest, "to reinforce the acceptance of diversity as a basis of cooperation."

Meanwhile, the possibility that solutions might be imposed on smaller, weaker states by larger, more powerful regimes continues to loom large in the ASEAN viewfinder, as concern remains that the United States, either unilaterally or with allies, might choose to forcefully in-tervene in yet another country, on a pretext related to the defense of human rights.

CONTRADICTION OF TWO NORMS

The critical issue in any debate on humanitarian intervention is the need to harmonize intervention with the principle of sovereignty, which in essence requires that a sovereign state be treated as an independent political unit, its territorial integrity be respected, and it be allowed to pursue its domestic affairs without external interference. These stipulations are essentially those regulating inter-state relations that have evolved since the Treaty of Westphalia and have been codified as core principles of international law.

In terms of intra-state affairs, however, sovereignty represents the result of a social contract between the government and the governed/ citizens to ensure good governance. Some of the intra-state components of sovereignty already have been embedded in humanitarian norms—such as in the case of the United Nations' 1948 Universal Declaration of Human Rights, the Genocide Convention of 1948, and the four Geneva Conventions signed in 1949—but it is only in the post–cold war world that democracy, human rights, and the rule of law have been recognized by the international community as principles ensuring good governance with legitimacy and accountability.

It is against this background that the debate on the legitimacy of humanitarian intervention must be continued, in order to clarify whether military intervention can be justified on the basis of general international law.

2. China

Jia Qingguo

THE tenor of international discourse has changed considerably since the end of the cold war, and debate has intensified regarding the legitimacy and desirability of international intervention, particularly when it involves the use of force. Opinions ran high in 1999 when, forces having been dispatched to the Federal Republic of Yugoslavia by the North Atlantic Treaty Organisation (NATO) to stop the genocide allegedly taking place in Kosovo, those very military operations caused the death of hundreds of Yugoslav civilians and serious destruction of the country's infrastructure and economy. This act of international intervention highlighted some striking contradictions.

Proponents of international intervention argue that it is necessary for both moral and practical reasons. Morally, the international community simply cannot ignore gross violations of human rights; human justice and compassion demand action to stop them. In this age of globalization, moreover, with events in individual countries increasingly affecting the interests of others, human rights violations in any one country threaten not only to bring about political unrest and rebellion in that country, but also to cause national security concerns, economic disruption, as well as refugee and other problems for its neighbors. Accordingly, in its own interests, the international community needs to take steps to stop violations of human rights wherever they may occur.

Ironically, those who oppose international intervention are also motivated by moral and practical considerations. They believe that international intervention is morally unjustifiable because it is a one-way activity: intervention of strong states in the affairs of the weak. Further, it is wrong to assume that strong states are always right in taking the moral high ground. Moreover, if intervention is accompanied by military force it causes bloodshed, and it hardly makes sense to commit a new wrong in order to address an old one. Not only that, but international intervention is often conducted to promote the selfish national interests of the intervening state, despite the lofty principles and goals it might espouse to justify its intervention. Finally, instead of promoting peace, stability, and progress, international intervention undermines national sovereignty, disrupts domestic and international order and, in the end, tends to complicate rather than lessen problems.

Basically, China does not favor international intervention, for which reason it has received much condemnation and ridicule from critics at home and abroad. Some have concluded that China is opposed to international intervention simply because, itself a gross violator of human rights, it wishes to perpetuate its authoritarian rule and, by defending national sovereignty, hopes to shield itself from international criticism.

This chapter argues that such an understanding fails to capture the complexity of the problem. Certainly one may disagree with the way China deals with particular domestic issues, but one nevertheless needs to understand the internal logic of its view on international intervention, and the historical constraints within which such a view has evolved. To this end, following a brief outline of China's official position on international intervention, especially of the military kind, the major factors that shape its views are identified. Finally, the chapter reflects on the proper conduct of international relations and international intervention.

POSITION OF THE CHINESE GOVERNMENT

Ever since the founding of the People's Republic of China in 1949, the Chinese government has opposed international intervention in its internal affairs. In a speech on October 1, 1949, Chinese leader Mao

Zedong cautioned that the imperialist powers would not accept the victory of China's revolution and would attempt to sabotage it and cause trouble, for which reason the Chinese people were to be on their guard (Mao 1977, 5). In a December 31, 1953, talk with an Indian official delegation, Chinese Premier and Foreign Minister Zhou Enlai proposed five basic rules by which the two countries should abide in handling their relations, including "mutual respect for each other's territorial integrity" and "non-interference in each other's internal affairs" (Zhou 1990, 63). These were later to become the five principles of peaceful coexistence advocated by China for proper international conduct.

Years later, in an October 31, 1989, talk with former U.S. President Richard Nixon, Chinese leader Deng Xiaoping said that the principle of noninterference in other countries' internal affairs should be upheld in international relations, and in a talk with the visiting Canadian prime minister on July 11, 1990, he said that China would never allow foreign countries to interfere in its internal affairs (Deng 1993, 332 and 359). In his speech at the Forum on China-Africa Cooperation on October 10, 2000, Chinese President Jiang Zemin said that the new international political and economic order should protect the sovereign equality of nation states and the rights of developing countries from foreign intervention in their internal affairs, stressing that no country has the right to either impose its social system and will on another country, or interfere in its internal affairs (Jiang 2000a).

In principle, China believes that its opposition to international intervention is consistent with internationally recognized standards of morality, international law, and pragmatism.

A One-Way Business

To begin with, international intervention has been a one-way business: In former times, imperialist and colonial powers intervened in other countries' internal affairs for domination and influence; today, strong Western countries interfere in developing countries' internal affairs for their own political, economic, and security interests. Since it more often than not serves the interests of the strong and damages the sovereign rights and interests of weaker states, reflecting Western domination of world affairs, international intervention should be resisted.

A Question of Legitimacy

Second, China believes that international intervention does not have
a legitimate political basis. At best, the government of the intervening
state is chosen by its own people, but neither by the international community nor the people of the target state. Accordingly, it has no legitimate authority to impose its political system and values on the people
of the target state. Also, it is arrogant to assume that the people of the
target state would welcome intervention; in many cases, the contrary is
true. Some may argue that a target state's government also lacks political legitimacy because it did not come to power through a competitive
and fair election. However, this lack on the part of the target state does
not legitimize intervention by other states.

Third, China believes that, under normal circumstances, international
intervention violates the Charter of the United Nations and international law, and so lacks legality. Chapter I, Article 2 of the UN Charter
upholds the principle of sovereign equality among member states. The
only chapter calling for international intervention—Chapter VII—
strictly limits its application to situations involving international military aggression. More important, the UN Charter specifically forbids
the threat or use of military force in conducting international relations
as being in violation of both the UN Charter and the territorial integrity and political independence of member states (Li 1993, 646–680).

In a September 7, 2000, comment on NATO's military intervention
in Kosovo, Jiang said that, in its efforts to reconcile and resolve international conflicts and strive for sustainable peace and common security, the international community should strictly observe the goals
and principles of the UN Charter and seek conflict resolution through
dialogue, negotiation, and consultation. The practice of bypassing the
UN Security Council, he noted, clearly goes against the will of the UN
member states, and the international community would do well to defend instead of undermine the authority of the UN Security Council,
and enhance rather than weaken its role (Jiang 2000b).

Self-interest Not Altruism

Fourth, China believes that, more often than not, international intervention is conducted to promote the interests of an intervening state

rather than those of the people of the target state. Such intervention is thus often characterized by double standards, selectiveness, and the cynical pragmatism of the intervening state's foreign policy, and can cause significant damage to the interests and self-respect of developing countries (Tian 1993, 571). In his comment on Western reactions to the 1989 Tiananmen Square incident, Deng pointed out that the West wanted to see problems in China, which was why some people in the United States talked about fighting even in the absence of a smoking gun (Deng 1993, 325–326). In a brief summary of the international situation, the Chinese Ministry of Foreign Affairs (2000) has compared the new style of international intervention with the gunboat diplomacy and economic colonialism of former times, and argues that this practice must be rejected.

Finally, China believes that international intervention usually causes more harm than good, even when it is conducted with the best intentions. On the human rights issue, for example, China argues that international intervention, in the form of confrontation and the exertion of pressure, is likely to exacerbate existing problems and spell disaster for target states (Liu 1996, 171). Many in China believe that Western interference in the internal affairs of the Soviet Union contributed to its collapse and the subsequent suffering experienced in Russia. According to the World Health Organization (WHO; 1997), the average life expectancy of Russians in 1994 was 57.7 years, some 10 years less than it had been before the collapse. If one were to calculate Russian life expectancy in terms of life lost, one could say that millions of lifetimes had been lost. And this human calamity has not taken into account the misery and suffering endured by those Russians who managed to survive.

In sum, China believes that international intervention is often immoral, unjust, ill motivated, and counterproductive in terms of the proclaimed objectives. Accordingly, under normal circumstances and on most issues, it should be rejected by international society. However, despite its general objection to international intervention, China has not always rejected it in its foreign policy practice.

Policy Flexibility

During the early years of the republic, China supported revolutionary activities in Third World countries, especially in Asia. During the years when the South African government stubbornly held on to its apartheid policy, China joined the rest of the world in condemning and opposing it and even refused to have anything to do with the South African government during the years when China most needed international recognition, instead supporting antigovernment forces. Moreover, China refrained from criticizing U.S. intervention in Somalia in 1993, when the latter's government collapsed and the country experienced a bloody civil war. More recently, China has supported U.S. efforts to topple the Taliban government in Afghanistan, due to its connection with the Al Qaeda terrorist group led by Osama bin Laden. Today, however, China no longer promotes revolutionary activities abroad, although it continues to oppose racism, and is likely to support international intervention to restore peace and order in failed states.

In addition, China believes that international society should make efforts to promote the cause of human rights. As Jiang stated at a luncheon in New York on September 8, 2000, democracy, freedom, and human rights are common pursuits of humankind (Jiang 2000c). From the Chinese government's perspective, every country should work to further protect human rights within their borders. As far as China itself is concerned, the government has subscribed to many international treaties and covenants on the protection of human rights over the years, especially since it opened up to the outside world in the late 1970s. It has expressed its willingness to work with the people of Asia Pacific and the world, to promote the cause of human rights regionally and internationally (Jiang 2000d).

Cooperation, Equality, Mutual Respect

While endorsing international dialogue and cooperation in promoting human rights, China insists that such cooperation should be conducted strictly on the basis of equality and mutual respect. It argues that every country must work to improve its human rights situation, and none should assume moral superiority and impose its preference on others. In promoting human rights in the world, countries must observe the five principles of peaceful coexistence, namely, mutual respect for territorial integrity, nonaggression, noninternational aggression, noninternational interference with domestic affairs, mutual benefit, and peaceful coexistence (Zhou 1990, 63).

China believes that international intervention and even international military intervention may, however, proceed in certain special and isolated cases when it becomes absolutely necessary—such as when a government practices blatant racism at home, collapses, and the country falls prey to uncontrolled domestic violence, or kills its own people en masse. However, even then, UN Security Council authorization should be obtained, as no state or group of states has the right to take matters into its own hands.

Further, China argues that one should understand human rights in a comprehensive way, rather than just focus on civil and political rights as some in the West have done when evaluating a country's human rights record. Consideration should be given to a country's level of economic development and historical background. While every country should protect human rights, each country has the right to determine how to do so in light of its economic, social, political, and cultural priorities (Information Office 1991, 67–70). While countries may voice their opinions on human rights situations in other countries, they should do so in a responsible way, avoid politicizing the issues, and not try to force their views on others.

Finally, China believes that, in promoting human rights, the international community should also take into account diversity in cultural practices and preferences. There is no need to strive for complete uniformity even on the question of human rights as long as fundamental principles are observed. International society should allow individual states leeway to improve human rights conditions in their countries, bearing in mind their respective historical backgrounds and cultural traditions for, as Jiang points out, "Ours is a diverse and colorful world. To ask all countries to institute the same political system and to judge the various choices made by the people of various countries according to the values of one country are not democratic at all" (Jiang 2000c).

THE SHAPING OF CHINA'S POSITION

China's stance on international intervention is based on four factors: the nature of the existing international system; China's experience with the outside world in modern times; its international status; and its domestic politics.

Despite what is being said about globalization and how it has changed the world, the international system remains one based on nation-states. As such, the system is both anarchic, in that it does not have an international authority such as a world government, and largely state-centric, with nation-states considered responsible for the welfare of their citizens and accountable for what happens within their borders. National governments draw their legitimacy primarily from their respective states, to which they accord their loyalty, responsibility, and accountability. It is on the basis of nation-states and national governments that international law, international norms, and international governmental organizations are defined. In terms of a world government, the United Nations would seem to most closely resemble such a body, although it lacks political authority, financial resources, and enforcement capabilities independent of its member states, as well as binding responsibilities and accountability to nonmember states.*

The nature of the international system and domestic politics necessitates that national governments defend national interests, including national sovereignty. The behavior of nation-states reflects domestic popular disposition more than anything else, particularly in the case of the United States. As the dominant world power, it places priority on domestic politics, not international law or international public opinion. The most recent example of such behavior is Washington's determination to build a National Missile Defense (NMD) system despite widespread international opposition. Even the European Union (EU), where supranational authority has evolved further than in any other region, is a product of the will of the people of individual states, rather than that of a united, European community. The bottom line is that states assert their sovereign rights in their own separate ways, for which reason China, like many other states, upholds national sovereignty.

If, under the existing international system, China asserts its national sovereignty, it is in part because its historical experience in foreign relations in modern times has made doing so imperative. During the century following the Opium War in 1840, China repeatedly suffered invasion and humiliation at the hands of foreign powers. In addition

*The concept of an international community is often seriously misrepresented. While the UN General Assembly may well be the body most closely resembling an international community, the term is often loosely and incorrectly used to refer merely to other countries or even groups of people that share the speaker's views.

to losing its former central, preeminent position in the world, it also lost control over territory and its destiny as foreign powers took over control of land and imposed their will on the rulers of China. In part because of this, China descended to the bottom rung of international society. Confronted with this stark reality, China has been trying to regain control over its destiny, through the process of modernization. In doing so, it has found the Western concept of national sovereignty useful, because it gives China the right to choose a way of modernizing befitting its circumstances.

Moreover, during the first 20 years following the founding of the republic, some Western countries, led by the United States, began to adopt a hostile policy of isolation and containment directed at China. Since then, in an effort to combat communism, they have tried to topple the Chinese government through overt and covert political, economic, and military endeavors. There are individuals and groups in the West who, for ideological or practical interests, have tried to sabotage China's development in the guise of promoting human rights and democracy. Since China's political institutions are still relatively weak because the country is in the midst of a drastic socioeconomic and political transformation, these attempts pose serious threats to China's political stability and the welfare of its people.

Against this background, the Chinese see national sovereignty as a useful tool to demonstrate equal standing in the family of nations in terms of equality and the respect it is due. They perceive international intervention in Chinese affairs as demeaning and undermining the country's self-respect, since such activity lends undue moral superiority to hostile foreign forces, giving them the opportunity to promote their interests and priorities at the expense of those of the Chinese people. It is, they believe, by adhering to the principle of national sovereignty that China can best defend its legitimate interests in international relations.

Its international status has also made it necessary for China to reject international intervention. Despite the tremendous progress it has made since 1949, especially since the reforms begun in 1978, China remains a relatively underdeveloped and weak country. Its economy still backward, politics under-institutionalized, and military capabilities inadequate to defend its legitimate interests, China finds itself on the receiving end of international intervention. Under the circumstances, were international intervention legitimized, China would be an even more likely target of international intervention. Chinese people do not generally believe that foreign intervention serves China's best interests, with the exception of those individuals and groups, such as separatists and religious fundamentalists, who harbor extravagant ambitions that the Chinese government cannot satisfy, and find support amongst anti-China foreign interests.

The Bumpy Road to Transition

Finally, domestic political considerations have made it both a necessity and an imperative that China rejects international intervention in its internal affairs. China is currently undergoing three fundamental transitions, namely, modernization, systemic transformation from a central planned economy to a market one, and a leadership transition from a generation of charismatic leaders to one of techno-bureaucrats. Modernization by nature is a very destabilizing process, because it involves rapid and fundamental changes in redistribution and social ethics. Many in society find it hard to adjust to such changes while, as Ted Gurr, political scientist and distinguished professor at the University of Maryland, points out, during a period of economic takeoff, some people develop a sense of relative deprivation because their expectations of social and economic benefits have far outstripped reality. This begets a sense of frustration that provides fodder for social and political unrest if not rebellion.

Systemic transition is also a very disruptive process, during which the central planned economy and the market economy exist side by side. Since these systems stand for two different principles of distribution and moral codes of conduct, people caught in the transition cannot but feel frustrated and, often, angry. Those people associated with the central planned sectors often complain about what they perceive to be the outrageous incomes of those in the market sectors and lament the increasing selfishness and greed seen in society. Meanwhile, those associated with the market sectors are highly critical of the power and privileges enjoyed and the persistence of what they consider to be the irrational ethics of the old days. The direct victims of the transition, such as unemployed workers of the state sectors, have even more grounds to be bitter. If not appropriately handled, the frustration and discontent may well translate into social and political unrest and rebellion. What has happened in eastern European countries since the collapse of the former Soviet Union may be the logical consequence of just such domestic political considerations and systemic transitions.

Leadership transitions are no less destabilizing. Charismatic leaders derive their power from either bloodlines or historical feats, such as the founding of a state. Power is invested in charismatic leaders, while political institutions only play a supportive role, for which reason one sees strong individuals and weak institutions. In contrast, techno-bureaucratic leaders derive their power from political institutions: These institutions possess the power and individual leaders exercise powers defined thereby. Hence, one finds strong institutions and weak leaders. Either type of leadership can be stable, but this is not so during periods of transition. When charismatic leaders pass away and techno-bureaucratic leaders take over, both leaders and institutions are weak, with political authority highly vulnerable to challenges and political stability fragile at best. China is going through this stage of transition.

Since China is currently simultaneously going through the three destabilizing transitions, the government is very concerned about political stability. In general, the Chinese people share the government view that priority should be given to preserving stability, the bedrock on which economic development and political progress depend. At this juncture, foreign intervention is believed to be disruptive, destructive and, therefore, unwanted.

In sum, the nature of the international system, China's experience with foreign relations in modern times, its current position in the international community, and its domestic political considerations have helped shape its position against international intervention. Thus, although China may be flexible on international intervention under certain specific conditions, unconditional endorsement is unlikely in the near future.

Over the longer term, however, China's position may evolve, making the country more receptive to international intervention as foreign relations become more beneficial, its position in the international community improves, and it successfully completes its current transitions.

However, even should that happen, China is likely to take a cautious approach. Its own experience, sense of justice, and previously stated principles will demand restraint.

INTERNATIONAL INTERVENTION: REFLECTIONS ON CHINA'S POSITION

The above analysis of China's position on international intervention should provide good reason to reflect on what might constitute proper international conduct. In studying international relations, it is necessary to avoid taking a black-and-white approach toward international intervention. Because of the complexity of the world, international intervention often involves contradictory and even conflicting moral claims and practical interests: Some may have good moral and practical reasons to engage in international intervention, while the targets of such intervention may have good moral and practical reasons to reject it.

Since the forces that drive countries differ, it is only natural that they should take different positions on such important issues as international intervention, for where one stands depends on where one sits. In terms of international intervention, a country's situation to a large extent determines its perception thereof. For stronger, more developed countries largely free of international intervention in their own internal affairs, legitimizing international intervention would not involve loss of independence, sovereignty, or people's welfare. However, in the case of weaker, developing countries, legitimizing international intervention entails loss of, or damage to, independence, sovereignty, political stability, and people's welfare. These are precisely the concerns of the Chinese government.

Certainly, if one genuinely wishes to promote international justice and progress, one should begin with demonstrating some sensitivity to, and understanding of, the different and often subtle concerns of the states involved, rather than just focus on those of one's own country. Such sensitivity is indispensable for the promotion of international justice and progress, and to minimize the negative impact this may entail. Only by showing sensitivity to, and understanding of, the problems others are facing is it possible to gain the cooperation rather than the resistance of developing countries such as China in efforts designed to promote international justice. In the final analysis, only through co-operation can international justice and progress be realistically advanced.

This, of course, does not mean that the international community should just take a hands-off approach, looking the other way when gross violations of human rights unfold. On the contrary, it should take a more proactive approach under the circumstances. However, in so doing, the international community should develop a set of criteria for intervention and the procedures whereby it should be conducted.

Given the fact that the current international system assigns the primary responsibility of taking care of the people to national governments, the principle of national sovereignty should be observed. Accordingly, international intervention should not be a routine affair. Rather, it should be conducted only under exceptional circumstances, such as when a national government practices racist policies, kills its people en masse, or collapses only to leave slaughtered people in its wake.

Under the current international arrangement, only the United Nations can represent the international community. While some countries may be sincere in their desire to promote international justice, their primary responsibility is to serve the interests of their own people and they do not have the authority to act on behalf of the international community. The United Nations, therefore, should determine, on the basis of the UN Charter and international law, whether a particular situation requires intervention and how the international community should intervene. It is true that the United Nations is often divided and can be very inefficient even once it has decided to act. However, given the alternatives, a UN response is more legitimate and causes less unwanted consequences in the long run. Those countries that really want to enhance the ability of international society to respond to human rights disasters should work to reform and strengthen the United Nations, rather than take matters into their own hands.

BIBLIOGRAPHY

Chinese Ministry of Foreign Affairs. 2000. "Zhongguo dui dangqian guofi xingshi de kanta" (China's view of the international situation). <http://www.fmprc.gov.cn/chn/2873.html>.

Deng Xiaoping. 1993. *Deng Xiaoping wenxuan* (Selected works of Deng Xiaoping), vol. 3. Beijing: Renmin Publishing House.

Information Office of the State Council of the People's Republic of China. 1991. *Zhongguo de renquan zhuangkuang* (China's human rights situation). Beijing: Information Office of the State Council.

Jiang Zemin. 2000a. "China and Africa: Usher in the New Century Together." Speech to the Forum on China-Africa Cooperation (translation). Beijing, 10 October. <http://www.fmprc.gov.cn/eng.5842.html> (3 October 2002).

———. 2000b. "Address at the UN Security Council Summit Meeting: President Jiang Zemin of the People's Republic of China" (translation). New York, 7 September. <http://www.un.org/sc/statements/chinae.htm> (2 October 2002).

———. 2000c. "Together to Build a China-U.S. Relationship Oriented Towards the New Century" (translation). Speech at a luncheon. New York, 8 September. <http://www.ncuscr.org/articles%20and%20speeches/jiang.speech.htm> (26 September 2002).

———. 2000d. Jiang Zemin zhi di ba jie yatai renquan yantaohui de hexin (Jiang Zemin's congratulatory letter to the eighth Asia-Pacific human rights seminar), 1 March. <http://big5.xinhuanet.com/gate/big5/news.xinhuanet.com/ziliao/2003-01/20/content_697319.htm>.

Li Tiecheng. 1993. *Lianheguo de licheng* (United Nations chronicles). Beijing: Beijing Yuyuan Xueyuan Publishing House.

Liu Liandi, ed. 1996. *Zhongmei guanxi zhongyao wenxian ziliao xuanbian* (Selected documents of Sino-American relations). Beijing: Shishi Publishing House.

Mao Zedong. 1977. *Mao Zedong xuanji* (Selected works of Mao Zedong), vol. 5. Beijing: Renmin Publishing House.

Tian Zengpei, ed. 1993. *Gaige kaifang yilai de zhongguo waijiao* (Chinese foreign policy since the adoption of the reforms and openness policy). Beijing: Shijie Zhishi Publishing House.

World Health Organization. 1997. "Life Expectancy at Birth Plummets in the Countries of the Former Soviet Union." Press Release WHO/13, 14 February. <http://www.who.int/archives/inf-pr-1997/en/pr97-13.html>.

Zhou Enlai. 1990. *Zhou Enlai waijiao wenxuan* (Selected works of Zhou Enlai on diplomacy). Beijing: Zhongyang Wenxian Publishing House.

3. Japan

Murata Kōji

WHETHER military intervention for humanitarian purposes is permissible is a vexed question that has been much debated since the North Atlantic Treaty Organisation (NATO) air strikes against the Federal Republic of Yugoslavia in 1999. By extension, one may ask whether the principles of state sovereignty are violated when outside military intervention aims to halt the actions either of a government that is engaged in grave infringements of human rights or responsible for the mass murder of its citizens, or of a country engulfed in civil war. Or, whether under certain circumstances, such intervention could be considered permissible under certain conditions.

While numerous studies on the subject of military intervention have been conducted in Japan and other countries over the past few years, the terrorist attacks in the United States on September 11, 2001, Washington's subsequent military campaign in Afghanistan, and the U.S. military action against Iraq have made all the more urgent the need to reconsider both the use of force in international politics and the concept of state sovereignty.[1]

This chapter first surveys changes in the international situation that have led to a growing call for humanitarian military intervention, before examining how Japan is handling recent developments and concomitant challenges.

TRENDS IN INTERNATIONAL POLITICS

The world system established under the Treaty of Westphalia in 1648 drew a sharp distinction between the anarchy that would reign among those states in international society that lack strong sovereign government, and the hierarchy of domestic society in which a government exercises ultimate power.[2] But this distinction was not strictly observed as international law and organizations were established and ultimate authority, even in domestic society, was not always unilateral. Then, in the latter half of the twentieth century, as interdependence among nations deepened, ties between international and domestic politics grew increasingly strong. This phenomenon came to be described as "intermestic," a term coined in the 1970s by combining the words international and domestic.

END OF THE COLD WAR

The acceleration of these trends toward greater interdependence and closer ties following the end of the cold war served to encourage humanitarian military intervention. According to Fujiwara Kiichi (2001b), the situation was the product of a shift in power politics, from mutual to unilateral deterrence, and the transition to parliamentary democracy in various parts of the world.

With the collapse of the Soviet Union, there ended the historical mission of the mutually assured destruction (MAD) defense strategy that had prevailed between Washington and Moscow, leaving the United States as the sole superpower. Then, with the so-called revolution in military affairs (RMA), U.S. military preeminence was further enhanced, leading to the emergence of the present regime, in which the United States intervenes to resolve regional conflicts and disturbances to international order, either on its own or at the head of a multinational force. This makes it unlikely that humanitarian intervention in the Third World by the United States or other Western nations will invite counter-intervention by, for example, Russia or China. As a matter of fact, even the United Nations Security Council could not prevent the United States from taking military action against Iraq in 2003 without a new resolution clearly authorizing the action. As Fujiwara points out, with military power thus concentrated in one place, "military action has become *police action*" (2001b, 113). Ideally, legitimate coercion in domestic politics is conducted by the police and, in international politics, by the military. In the former case, peace is maintained through a monopoly on, or concentration of, coercive force; in the latter, stability and balance among countries is achieved through the dispersal of armed force. Today, however, with the U.S. military predominant in international politics, its international political role has increasingly come to resemble that of a domestic police force.

In post–cold war world politics, threats to national security in the United States from such sources as terrorism and drug trafficking have led to an overlap in the jurisdictions of the military and the police, resulting in the internationalization and militarization of police activities, as has been vividly demonstrated by September 11 and subsequent related events (Fujiwara 2001b, 112–113).

Democratization has made great progress in east Asian countries, which have seen remarkable economic growth since the 1970s, while in eastern Europe the democratic process has been spreading rapidly since the collapse of the Soviet Union. But that has not brought about the end of history, as Francis Fukuyama (1992) predicted. Although many countries are still not equipped to exercise parliamentary democracy, it has become increasingly difficult to flatly reject such fundamental values of democracy as freedom of speech, respect for human rights, and the right to free elections.

THEORY OF DEMOCRATIC PEACE

The influential theory currently circulating among political scientists in the United States is that of democratic peace, according to which war is believed to be highly unlikely to occur between liberal democracies (Russett 1993). This is despite the fact that, since the collapse of the Soviet Union, the United States and its Western allies no longer have an outside military threat that solidifies their alliance. Thus, there is room for attention to swing to the common values of human rights, freedom of speech, and democracy. Simply put, while American military superiority makes humanitarian military intervention possible, the spread of democratic values often elicits such intervention.

It is important to note that, after the cold war, the first U.S. president was the Democrat Bill Clinton, and that social democrats came to power in major western European countries thereafter as well. Generally, the U.S. Democratic Party and European social democratic parties are more optimistic regarding social reform, more sensitive to fundamental human rights, and more tolerant of big government (and, therefore, big military spending) than are conservative parties.

Thus, while the Clinton administration attempted to spread democracy by, for example, its policy of engagement with China, the George W. Bush administration is giving priority to national interests and the perception that there are threats from abroad. (Recently, however, under the so-called neo-conservatives, the Bush administration tends to emphasize a regime change in other countries, if necessary.) This stance does not, however, run counter to the American desire to establish a political community based on universal principles, for it seeks to strengthen the sense of community with its allies and friendly nations. Simply put, the difference between the Clinton and Bush administrations is that of emphasizing the expansion[3] or the solidarity of that political community (Hosoya 2001, 6). The criticism of the United States being voiced today is that, backed by the overwhelming military power and economic superiority of the nation, Bush is engaging in even more unilateral policies than his predecessors.[4]

ROLE OF THE MASS MEDIA

Here one should, perhaps, consider the expanding role of the mass media. In the area of humanitarian military intervention, the media's role is a double-edged sword. On the one hand, the spread of the media, especially television networks, has made it possible to transmit instantly and vividly to people's living rooms everywhere any incident that might occur in any part of the world. An atrocity committed in an obscure part of a country can no longer be so easily dismissed as someone else's business by those in other countries. Figuratively speaking, humankind is facing not the end of history but, rather, "the end of geography" (Inoguchi 2002, 236).

On the other hand, the growth of the mass media has made the public better informed concerning the costs and risks involved in military intervention. Former Secretary of State James A. Baker, who played a prominent role during the Gulf War, has noted that the United States is not indifferent to developments in world affairs but, as the sole superpower, can neither nip in the bud nor solve all the knotty problems that arise in the world. U.S. leaders, Baker believes, must thus choose which problems to tackle on the basis of national interest as well as American principles and values. He remarks that the constant worldwide transmission of video images by satellite broadcasts makes it difficult to be appropriately selective (Baker and DeFrank 1995).

In the Vietnam War, it is said, the United States was defeated not in the jungles of Indochina but in the living rooms of U.S. households. Partly aided by the rising awareness of human rights, public opinion in the United States became sensitive to the loss of even a few servicemen. That trend was also seen during the 1992–1994 U.S. engagement in Somalia, which ended with the withdrawal of U.S. troops after the lives of 36 U.S. soldiers were lost. Since then, the U.S. military has adhered to a no-casualties principle of engagement. Today, the American public is becoming more and more sensitive to the increasing number of American casualties in occupied Iraq.

The spread and development of the mass media is conducive to both facile military intervention and withdrawal. High expectations are pinned on the development of precision-guided weapons developed as a result of the RMA, with the cost and risks of military intervention reduced as high-tech, clean wars are conducted centering on air strikes —as opposed to dirty wars that rely on ground warfare, which inevitably involves heavy casualties. However, a war is only defined as clean by the intervening party; casualties caused by misaimed or stray bombs and other collateral damage are never insignificant for the victims, as has been seen in Kosovo, Afghanistan, and Iraq. Events in such theaters of conflict make use of the term humanitarian difficult to justify.

In post–cold war international politics, the factors that make humanitarian military intervention both possible and necessary have become increasingly important. A growing number of persuasive voices are being raised opposing the hegemony of the United States, calling for diverse interpretations of democracy and human rights, and condemning the inhumane impact of humanitarian military intervention.

JAPAN'S RESPONSE TO INTERVENTION

Japan's Constitution is known as a peace constitution for the content of Article 9, which states:

> Aspiring sincerely to an international peace based on justice and order, the Japanese people forever renounce war as a sovereign right of the nation and the threat or use of force as means of settling international disputes.
>
> In order to accomplish the aim of the preceding paragraph, land, sea, and air forces, as well as other war potential, will never be maintained. The right of belligerency of the state will not be recognized.

Open to various interpretations, Article 9 has been a major issue in post–World War II Japanese politics (Nakamura 2001; Murata 2000). Among scholars of constitutional law there are two main schools of thought concerning this article. One holds that the Self-Defense Forces (SDF) are unconstitutional, because the first paragraph of the article proscribes war. The other maintains that the first paragraph prohibits only wars of aggression, but that, because the second paragraph renounces the maintenance of war potential, the SDF are unconstitutional.

Meanwhile, the current interpretation of the Japanese government is that the article does *not* prohibit possession of the minimum necessary capability for the exercise of self-defense, since the first paragraph of Article 9 prohibits only wars of aggression, while the second paragraph commences with the proviso, "[i]n order to accomplish the aim of the preceding paragraph . . . ."

That still does not define the right to collective self-defense or clarify the issues surrounding the dispatch of SDF personnel overseas.

Collective Self-Defense

According to Article 51 of the Charter of the United Nations, the right of individual or collective self-defense is an inherent right of member countries. Similar statements are found in Article 5 of the San Francisco Peace Treaty and the preamble of the U.S.-Japan Security Treaty. When the latter treaty was revised in 1960, then-Prime Minister Kishi

Nobusuke stated in the Diet: "[Japan's] provision of military bases to another country and jointly defending itself with that country has been correctly interpreted as exercise of the right to collective self-defense. I believe that Japan has such a right as a matter of course" (Sase 2001). He thus understood that allowing U.S. military bases on Japanese soil under the U.S.-Japan Security Treaty in a broad sense constituted the exercise of the right to collective self-defense.

However, the understanding of the government subsequently changed, as can be seen from a document it submitted in 1972 in response to an opposition interpolation in the Diet: "The government has consistently held the position that although [Japan] has what is called in international law the right to collective self-defense [it] cannot exercise that right as a sovereign right of the nation because it would overstep the bounds of self-defense permitted in the Constitution . . ." (Sase 2001, 130).

Further, in a written reply in 1981 the government states: "It is only natural, according to international law, that inasmuch as it is a sovereign state, Japan should have the right to collective self-defense. [The government] understands, however, that exercising the right to self-defense under Article 9 of the Constitution must be limited to the minimum extent necessary for defense of the nation and that exercising the right to collective self-defense would exceed that limit and not be permitted under the Constitution" (Sase 2001, 125). According to the 1972 and 1981 interpretations of the article, Japan has the right to collective self-defense but cannot exercise it.

"By any world standard," writes Kitaoka Shin'ichi (2002, 25) of the University of Tokyo, "providing military bases to another country constitutes exercise of the right to collective self-defense. Japan, however, narrowly interprets exercise of the right to collective self-defense and regards such exercise as unconstitutional (and other activities as constitutional). What the Koizumi Jun'ichirō Cabinet did was to even further narrow the interpretation of this right, formulating the idea that extending cooperation to foreign troops in the form of transportation of supplies did not amount to exercise of the right of collective self-defense."

Kitaoka also argues that not exercising the right to collective self-defense is a wrong option militarily, in that Japan should maintain a military capability for the purpose of self-defense. As he points out, rejection of the right to collective self-defense is a diplomatic blunder, as a result of which each time Japan does something that transcends its definition of the right to individual self-defense, it must provide an explanation for its action. Further, he argues, it is illogical that, while the Cabinet Legislation Bureau supports the possession of defense capabilities, it should see the right to individual self-defense as being safer than the right to collective self-defense (Kitaoka 1999, 31). The government interpretation that Japan has the right to collective self-defense but cannot exercise it is unconvincing.

History Constrains Resolve

The repeated sending of troops abroad by the pre–World War II government in the name of "self-existence and self-defense," led the nation to devastation. When the Defense Agency Establishment Law and the Self-Defense Forces Law were enacted in 1954, the House of Councillors adopted a resolution prohibiting the dispatch of SDF troops outside Japanese territory. The resolution was brief: "On the occasion of the establishment of the Self-Defense Forces, the House hereby reconfirms, in the light of relevant articles of the Constitution and the Japanese people's earnest devotion to peace, that no SDF troops will be dispatched overseas" (Tanaka 1997, 140). The resolution was not binding, but it did reflect the sentiments of Japanese people in those days. At the time, Japan was not a member of the United Nations, so there was no suggestion that the SDF might contribute to the maintenance of international peace by joining UN-sponsored peacekeeping operations (PKO).

In July 1958, after Japan joined the United Nations, UN Secretary-General Dag Hammarskjold called on the Japanese government to send SDF personnel to join a UN observer group. In response, UN Ambassador Matsudaira Kōtō made a controversial comment in the *Yomiuri Shimbun* vernacular newspaper: "Some people in Japan advocate the strengthening of UN diplomacy, but from my experience I believe that what other countries in the world want Japan to do is to send SDF units to serve in the Congo [and elsewhere] as part of UN forces. Under the Constitution the dispatch of troops overseas is considered impossible, but SDF personnel should be sent at least as observers. I believe that in the future [SDF personnel] should be part of a UN police force as well." Prime Minister Ikeda Hayato had to promptly repudiate the comment, saying, "UN Ambassador Matsudaira's statement that the basic way of cooperating with the United Nations is to join the UN police force is mistaken" (Tanaka 1997, 210–211).

It was not until the early 1990s that the Japanese government made any real effort to take part in PKO activities. The Persian Gulf crisis in 1990 and the Gulf War in the following year were the first real challenge to international security following the end of the cold war. The Japanese government drafted the UN Peace Cooperation Bill, but it failed to be passed in the Diet. So, despite its reliance on Middle Eastern oil and its alliance with the United States, Japan could not even cooperate in the transportation of supplies, and was only able to give financial assistance. Then, when Tokyo contributed the huge amount of US$13 billion, it was ridiculed overseas for its checkbook diplomacy. When Japan was finally able to send minesweepers to the Gulf, the war was already over.

"People's perceptions of security [at that time]," recalls Iokibe Makoto of Kobe University, "had not progressed beyond the heated and ideological debates of the 1950s, a time of black-and-white arguments over whether it was to be war or peace, revival of militarism or democracy, aggression or self-defense. The lexicon of the Japanese postwar mentality included only two types of war: wars of aggression and wars of self-defense" (1999, 229). For Japan, however, the Gulf War was neither a war of aggression nor of self-defense. While it should have been a matter of international security, Japan failed to promptly and properly respond.

Views on Peacekeeping Involvement Change

With the diplomatic setbacks of the Gulf War behind it, the Miyazawa Kiichi Cabinet enacted the Law concerning Cooperation for United Nations Peacekeeping Operations and Other Operations (International Peace Cooperation Law; so-called PKO Law) in June 1992. Several circumstances made this possible.

First, the influential ruling Liberal Democratic Party (LDP) politician Ozawa Ichirō and other party members were eager that the PKO bill be passed even at the risk of endangering the support base of the Miyazawa cabinet. Second, the government had around that time begun to officially express the hope that Japan might be granted permanent membership of the UN Security Council. Third, Japan, as an Asian power, had every intention of participating in the imminent UN peacekeeping operations in Cambodia. And fourth, China, which had been isolated internationally since the Tiananmen Square incident of 1989, had indicated it would not protest the enactment of the PKO Law in order to smooth the way for a visit by the Japanese Emperor to commemorate the twentieth anniversary of the normalization of Sino-Japanese diplomatic ties.

The law stipulated five prerequisites for Japan's participation in peacekeeping activities overseas. First, a cease-fire agreement was to be reached among the parties to armed conflicts; second, consent was to be obtained from the host countries and parties to the armed conflict for Japan's participation; third, operations would have to be strictly impartial and not favor any of the parties to the armed conflict; fourth, should any of the previous three requirements cease to be satisfied, the Japanese government could withdraw its SDF units; and fifth, the use of weapons was to be limited to the minimum necessary to protect the lives of SDF personnel.

The opposition parties were not, however, satisfied with these strictures. The then Social Democratic Party of Japan resisted passage of the law by adopting the vote-delaying tactic, known as the ox walk, of inching toward the Diet ballot box at a snail's pace. The Democratic Socialist Party (DSP), meanwhile, demanded that Diet approval be obtained before SDF personnel were sent overseas; and the Kōmeitō (Clean Government Party) demanded that a freeze be put on Japanese participation in UN peacekeeping forces (PKF) until public consensus had been reached.

The ruling LDP accepted these demands, as a result of which the overseas activities in which the SDF could engage were limited to the provision of medical services, transportation, telecommunications, and construction. In addition, the problem regarding the use of weapons remained, the decision on their use being left to individual discretion.

At the time of the Gulf crisis, when the government had submitted the UN Peace Cooperation Bill to the Diet, it was strongly opposed by the public, but in 1992 arguments were also advanced for the new bill. After it was enacted, SDF personnel joined the PKO in Cambodia and fulfilled their mission there. A poll conducted by the *Yomiuri Shimbun* newspaper in June 1993 shows that 56 percent of the respondents favored Japan's participation in the PKO (Tanaka 1997, 322). However, when a member of Japan's police force and a civilian Japanese volunteer were killed, Miyazawa recalls, "if even one more Japanese national had been killed the next day, [the operation] would have been finished. The situation was that tough. The Cabinet might have fallen had another person died" (2001, 74).

Subsequently, Japan accumulated experience in PKO participation, for which reason it is stated in the Guidelines for Japan-U.S. Defense Cooperation as revised in September 1997, that the two countries shall work together for peace and stability in Asia Pacific and the international community as a whole, in the areas of PKO and international humanitarian relief operations.

In June 1998, three areas of the PKO Law were revised on the basis of Japan's PKO experience. First, Japan's participation in the monitoring of elections overseas, formerly allowed only when such activities were related to UN peacekeeping operations, was in future to be permitted even when the United Nations and other regional organizations were involved in operations other than peacekeeping. Second, the requirements according to which Japan would extend contribution in kind for international humanitarian relief operations conducted by the Office of the United Nations High Commissioner for Refugees (UNHCR) or other international organizations, were eased so that assistance could be given even when agreement on a ceasefire had not been reached among the parties to the armed conflict. And third, in order to ensure more appropriate use of weapons, SDF personnel who had until then been left to use weapons at their own discretion, were now as a rule to obey the orders of their superiors in the field regarding weapons use.

In October 2001, only a month after the September 11 terrorist attacks on New York and Washington, D.C., the Japanese Diet approved the Anti-Terrorism Special Measures Law, and in December the 1992 PKO Law was amended a second time. These measures were taken in anticipation of the possible dispatch of SDF personnel to support reconstruction in Afghanistan, and to help in UN peacekeeping operations in East Timor. The December PKO Law amendments were designed, first, to lift the freeze on SDF participation in such PKF activities as monitoring ceasefires, disarming local forces, patrolling demilitarized zones, inspecting the transport of weapons, and collecting and disposing of abandoned weapons; second, to expand the scope of the activities in which members of the SDF are permitted to engage, so that rather than have use of weapons limited to self-defense or to defend the lives of other SDF members at the site when it is unavoidable, use was expanded to protection of those with whom the SDF work on site and others "under their control"; and, third, to allow the application of Article 95 of the Self-Defense Forces Law permitting weapons to be used for protection.

In this way, revisions have been gradually instituted in the PKO Law, and public support for participation in peacekeeping operations overseas has become well established. The five principles that are conditional for participation of Japanese SDF personnel, however, represent a high hurdle to the implementation of this policy. For example, Japan was not at first able to send SDF personnel to East Timor on peacekeeping duties, because it initially adhered strictly to the principle that there had to be an agreement on a ceasefire among the parties to the armed conflict. In 2002, under the revised PKO Law, 690 SDF personnel were stationed in East Timor.

Also, in July 2003 Japan decided to send SDF personnel to occupied Iraq. Because the Iraqi government disappeared after the war and did not accept any PKO, a new special law for dispatching SDF personnel to Iraq had to be passed. Under the new law, regulations concerning the use of weapons by the SDF are relaxed, but the SDF's activities are limited to non-combat areas, which are extremely difficult to define under the current situation in occupied Iraq.

STANCE ON INTERVENTION IN YUGOSLAVIA

Japan has overcome many obstacles over the past 10 years in an effort to make its PKO Law more effective, but when it comes to humanitarian intervention by force, the story is quite different. In March 1999, when NATO started to conduct air strikes against Yugoslavia, the Japanese government released a statement saying that it "understands [the strikes] as an unavoidable measure for humanitarian purposes" (Yanai 1999, 28). It went on to provide US$100 million for refugee assistance and aid to Albania and Macedonia, and another US$100 million for the UN Trust Fund for Human Security, to assist returned refugees after peace had been restored (Yanai 1999, 30). While Japan could not participate directly in PKF operations at that stage, it showed its readiness to cooperate along with other participating nations of the Group of Eight (G-8) and to cooperate mainly by giving economic support.

Public opinion within Japan was divided on NATO's humanitarian military intervention. Critic Yamazaki Masakazu wrote:

> At the beginning of the modern era, the clan and the village managed to survive by setting the individual free to move beyond their bounds and accepting the expanded powers of the state with which they identified. In the twenty-first century, as long as the state frees individuals to expand beyond itself and accepts globalization of the demand for human rights its existence will be accepted. Just as loyalty to the clan and to the village survived by coexistence with loyalty to the state, patriotism will only be able to survive by harmonizing itself with identity with humankind as a whole. The modern person who accepted constraints on the clan and the village must accept, by the same logic, constraint on the sovereignty of the state. (1999, 1)

Political scientist Tanaka also accepted the intervention by NATO, explaining it as follows.

> [I]n the latter half of the twentieth century, particularly from the 1990s, I think we can assume that the correlation between respect for human rights and the principle of nonintervention [in domestic affairs] evolved with the expansion of the former. This does not mean that intervention in the affairs of another nation is acceptable in just any case of infringement of human rights, however. It is a question, rather, of the large-scale and serious violation of human rights in which an immediate response is demanded. (2000, 61)

While noting that the NATO move had not been sanctioned by a resolution of the UN Security Council, Tanaka also argues:

> [T]he United Nations is an important system for seeking international security, but it is not a world government. The means and institutions for realizing the public good in a world system that is not a unitary state cannot be either one dimensional or

hierarchical. While the public good may sometimes be realized at the initiative of the United Nations, sometimes it may be the result of a consensus by the majority of states. (2000, 63)

In the case of the intervention in Kosovo, Tanaka says the G-8 framework functioned effectively, and constituted the "public good," as did the indictment of President Slobodan Milosevic by the International Criminal Tribunal for the former Yugoslavia, as well as the initiative of two non-NATO leaders—former Russian Prime Minister Viktor Chernomyrdin and Finnish President Martti Ahtisaari—in persuading Milosevic to surrender (Tanaka 2000, 66). Public good, he says, is created through such collective efforts.

Indeed, it is dangerous to place too much confidence in the United Nations, as Japanese are often inclined to do. Article 1 of the UN Charter says that its purpose is "to maintain international peace and security," but that only means the United Nations is a means for achieving that purpose. The power of any permanent member of the Security Council to veto resolutions, moreover, shows that the United Nations is by no means a thoroughly fair and egalitarian organization. The time China vetoed a motion to continue PKO activities in Macedonia and that nation subsequently succumbed to civil war is still fresh in our memories. Apparently, China's veto reflected its displeasure with the fact that Macedonia had established formal diplomatic relations with Taiwan (Tanaka 2000). The malfunction of the UN Security Council was again clearly demonstrated in the case of the war against Iraq.

Political scientist Ōnuma Yasuaki states categorically that "international society will not tolerate human rights infringement on the scale of the German Holocaust even if the nation in question protests that such action involves intervention in its domestic affairs. Today, no country, no despot, can ignore this principle" (1998, 91). And this, I might add, represents the general world consensus.

FORCES THAT MOTIVATE INTERVENTION

Not all humanitarian military intervention, however, can be justified. The conditions and means of intervention are extremely important. Specialists on regional affairs conversant with the local situation are generally cautious with regard to intervention. Sadakata Mamoru, one of Japan's few experts on the former Yugoslavia, for example, has made the stern comment:

> The problem with the humanitarian intervention in the Kosovo crisis was that it was not truly carried out for humanitarian considerations. First "there was intervention," and the idea that it was humanitarian was simply used in order to justify it.... To the United States, the crux of the problem was neither "nonintervention in the internal affairs" of a sovereign state nor was it "humanitarian intervention." At the Rambouillet talks, the United States called for either a NATO deployment within Yugoslavia or NATO airstrikes against targets there. The choice, then, was "internal intervention" or "military intervention." As far as Yugoslavia was concerned, where is there any room here for consideration from its point of view? (2000, 38)

Authority on German security affairs in Japan Iwama Yōko also observes that "We should avoid idealizing Kosovo as a model of humanitarian military intervention. We must recognize first of all that for the members of NATO, while defending human rights was indeed an important motive behind the strikes, that was certainly not the only consideration involved." Further, she expresses reservations, noting how the move resulted from "the need to prevent destabilization of the domestic affairs of [surrounding nations] resulting from the large influx of refugees [from Kosovo]." It involved "national interests, pure and simple." The Kosovo intervention was a case that elicited regional concern transcending state borders, she comments, but only on a very limited scale (Iwama 1999, 14–15). Needless to say, many specialists of Middle Eastern affairs, though they tend to hate the Saddam Hussein regime, are quite critical of the U.S. military action against Iraq.

Scholar of international law Mogami Toshiki reproves the impure motives and inhumane methods of the NATO strikes:

> While proclaiming their activity "humanitarian," NATO member countries did not rescue the victims of suffering, but punished the victimizer from afar instead, placing the safety of the reprisal force foremost. Punishing the victimizers can sometimes be effective, but one would think it was essentially more important to

rescue the victims of oppression, even if it meant the rescuers had to expose themselves to some degree of danger. It is not easy for people to make such a self-sacrifice, it goes without saying. But it is impossible to just evade what has to be done and resort to violent means, facilely labeling them "humanitarian." Herein lies the fullest proof that the bombing of Yugoslavia was not what one could call "humanitarian intervention." (2001, 126)

It does not seem feasible to consider Kosovo a model case of humanitarian intervention. Still, many fear that the United States, the world's sole superpower, is likely to launch further interventions of this kind.

Tanaka quotes influential American political scientists Joseph Nye, Richard Haas, and others, saying:

[T]he United States' role in the world order is decisive, but when we examine the U.S. national interest and its internal strategies toward the outside, I think the possibility is slim that the United States will repeatedly engage in the kind of military intervention we have seen in Kosovo for the purpose of upholding what it considers to be the universal principles of human rights. The condition of American action, is first, as Nye sees it, that U.S. interests are at stake, and second, as Haas says, its anticipation of forming a kind of international "police force" of countries willing to take on the task of assuring peace and order. U.S. unilateralism is a problem to watch out for, but when it comes to major infringements of human rights, hesitation to act is itself more a matter of concern than that sort of unilateral tendency. (2000, 69)

Tanaka notes that, in connection with the mistaken bombing of the Chinese embassy in Belgrade, more damage was done to Chinese national interests than might have otherwise been the case as a result of its refusal to accept the incident as a mistake and its strong denunciation of U.S. strategic intentions, which reflected Beijing's pursuit of power politics (2000, 280). Tanaka observes that those who opposed the bombing of Yugoslavia to the very end were the so-called realists, but, paradoxically, once NATO military intervention had begun, it could not be retracted (2000, 58).

Also, the possibility that the United States will again engage in the kind of military action it took against Iraq will not be so high because of the cost and repercussions in international public opinion. Given the difficulties of occupying Iraq now facing the United States, the so-called realists as well as the general public in the United States will be more reluctant for the country to take this kind of action again.

JAPANESE CONSTRAINTS

As the above views illustrate, the essence of the debate in Japan is that while observers agree that large-scale massacres such as those in Kosovo cannot be tolerated, they sharply disagree on the need for, and method of, military intervention, as well as regarding the U.S. response.

The so-called humanitarian military intervention is a particularly vexing issue for Japan. Some progress has been made over the past 10 years as Japan has laid the legal groundwork for participation in non-military endeavors justified under international law, such as peace-keeping operations. But when it comes to armed intervention, even if for humanitarian purposes, Japan is constrained by several considera-tions. With a view to obtaining a permanent seat on the UN Security Council, Japan needs to contribute to international society and, as one of Washington's chief allies, it is eager to cooperate with the United States. Yet, as a nation in Asia, in which region many countries are ex-periencing ethnic strife, and given that its pre-1945 history of interven-tion in the region is still remembered, Japan does not want to become isolated for having supported humanitarian military intervention. Under the present legal framework that makes it difficult to explicitly exercise the right of collective self-defense, Japan could not use force were it to take part in a humanitarian military mission.

One might well speak of the end of geography with reference to Kosovo, which is far removed from Japan both physically and in terms of cultural understanding. Moreover, a number of Europe-specific fac-tors figured in the turmoil there—the analogy with the Holocaust of Nazi Germany, the rethinking of the role of NATO in the post–cold war era, and national concerns as refugees spilled out of Yugoslavia. Insofar as Japan was made aware of the significance of humanitarian intervention in distant Kosovo, the concept of the end of geography failed to convince Tokyo that this was a problem truly requiring its involvement. This is also applicable to European countries, which felt a less direct security threat from Iraq than from Kosovo.

Furthermore, unlike most other Asian nations, Japan does not face the likelihood of being a target of outside humanitarian intervention, since it does not have the kind of serious ethnic confrontations within its borders that might elicit such action. Even by the standards of the West, Japan is a democratic nation that protects human rights. More-over, not having experienced the bloodshed and struggle that resulted in human rights and democracy being established in Europe and the United States, Japan is not very responsive when it comes to participa-tion in humanitarian military intervention.

As noted above, soon after the September 11 terrorist attacks in the United States, the Japanese Diet passed the Anti-Terrorism Special Measures Law that some, including a former head of the SDF Joint Staff Council, see as establishing a precedent for the exercise of collec-tive self-defense (Sakuma 2002). Given the scale of the terrorist assault, China did not voice the usual and expected opposition to this major change in Japan's security policy, much as had been the case in 1992, when Japan passed its PKO Law after the Gulf War had ended. Beijing's silence suggests the importance of the Asian factor in considering Tokyo's security policy. The fall 2001 response clearly shows how the trauma suffered by Japanese leaders at the time of the Gulf War had shaped their thinking 10 years on. For, while Europe and the United States in that time experienced a succession of grave international se-curity crises involving the large-scale exercise of military force, Japan had experienced little other than issues of national security, such as a North Korean ballistic missile passing over Japanese territory.[5] It should be noted, however, that the increasing military threat from North Korea makes the Japanese more and more sensitive to their na-tional security.

FUTURE CHALLENGES

The rights and wrongs of humanitarian military intervention cannot be discussed in abstract terms, since definitions depend, to a large extent, on the individual case. What is required is both the wisdom to discern what kind of humanitarian military intervention is acceptable under which conditions, and a record of the efforts made to enhance the legitimacy of Japan's position in case it should be involved in such intervention.

As for the criteria for intervention, Joseph Nye (1999) suggested the following: 1) The degree of intervention should reflect the degree of concern, and military intervention should be reserved for the most serious cases; 2) the use of force should be avoided unless both humanitarian and national interests are at stake; 3) there should be a clear grasp of what is meant by genocide; and 4) great care should be taken when intervening in civil wars waged in the interests of national self-determination.

Certainly even these criteria involve some arbitrariness, but criteria that are excessively narrow will rarely work in the real, complex world of international politics. Japan should formulate its own criteria, taking care not to bifurcate humanitarian and national interests.

Were Japan to wish to cooperate even indirectly in humanitarian military intervention, a UN Security Council resolution would go far in galvanizing the support of the Japanese public. Thus, in the wake of Washington's military action in Afghanistan following the September 11 attacks, 54 percent of those surveyed in Japan said they felt that a UN resolution should have been passed approving the U.S. action. The same survey reveals that comparable feelings were shared by 90 percent of the pollees in China and 15 percent of those in the United States. Many Japanese were suspicious about the legitimacy when the United States took military action against Iraq without a new UN resolution. However, as Tanaka argues, a UN Security Council resolution alone should not legitimize armed intervention. Japan tends to regard the United Nations as an absolute power, and has little awareness of its political nature and the arbitrariness of its decisions. Some influential opinion leaders in Japan expressed their negative views on the United Nations after the war against Iraq. It is important, therefore, that Japan should not only seek to be a permanent member of the Security Council, but that it also present a vision for a wide range of UN reforms.

It would seem inconceivable that Japan might support humanitarian military intervention by a single nation, no matter how predominant that nation's power might be. Generally, the degree to which intervention is perceived to be legitimate increases in direct proportion to the number of nations involved and how many nations support such action. Even in the case of the war against Iraq, more than 30 countries expressed direct support. If a regional organization supports intervention in a country within its bounds, the possibility that the intervention will succeed is quite high, although if a world power with interests in that region opposes intervention, the possibility of success is low.

Moreover, humanitarian intervention does not always equate with armed or state intervention. Were Japan to assist nongovernmental organizations (NGOs) engaged in humanitarian activities, they could reduce the need for humanitarian military intervention and play an important role in enhancing the legitimacy of Japan's position (Mogami 2001). In addition, Japan and Western nations should promote human rights within their own borders as well as the spread of democracy around the world.

While good progress has been made in establishing the legal apparatus for Japanese participation in overseas peacekeeping operations, the legitimacy of Tokyo's involvement depends on its contributions and efforts. Since regional disputes occur in specific historical and geographic contexts, Japan would be well advised to train properly informed specialists in the local history and affairs of unstable Third World areas.

The September 11 terrorist attacks and the U.S. military action against Iraq again brought to the fore criticisms and the deep-rooted distrust of America's unilateral actions, not only among Third World countries but also among European countries. The issue of humanitarian military intervention may only deepen such sentiments and make them more complex. "America's challenge [is] to recognize [our] own preeminence but to conduct . . . policy as if [we] were still living in a world of many centers of power," wrote Henry Kissinger, warning that even the greatest power would soon succumb to internal decay were it to behave otherwise (2001, 288).

One might argue that, to forestall both extreme unilateralism and a tendency to isolationism on the part of the United States, Tokyo should treat Washington as a friend and ally. To that end, the issue of collective self-defense must be addressed. Japan's postwar defense policy lacks direction, appearing only to be determined *not* to exercise the right to collective self-defense. If this is to change, Japan must clearly state what it has decided, in order to avoid triggering anxiety in other Asian countries. Since September 11, it has become increasingly evident that cooperation among allies and international security will increasingly overlap, as evidenced by the first declaration by NATO of its intention to exercise the right of collective self-defense. At the same time, however, the war against Iraq demonstrated the difficulties of maintaining a sound alliance relationship with the overwhelming power: the United States. If Japan is to avoid being torn between its obligations both as an ally of the United States and also as an Asian nation, it must declare its position on international security affairs.[6]

For Japan, the question of humanitarian military intervention is currently essentially only a matter of formulating its vision of diplomacy for the twenty-first century. While it does not immediately have to decide on the pros and cons of, or commit itself to, such intervention, Japan would be well served were it to debate the issue without further delay in anticipation that the need to do so may well suddenly arise.

NOTES

1. For an outstanding study of the use of force in international politics, see Craig and George (1995), especially chapters 19 and 20. Numerous writings have already been published about the September 11 terrorist attacks, amongst which is a recent and relatively balanced collection of essays in Japanese, written by liberal intellectuals in Japan and overseas in a volume edited by Fujiwara Kiichi (2001a), and an essential and highly informative essay written by Yamazaki Masakazu (2001) immediately after the attacks.

2. A philosophical study of the characteristics of international society can be found in Hedley Bull (1995).

3. The theoretical study of achieving security through expansion of the political community originated with Karl Deutsch (1975).

4. Many argue that Bush's stance is largely due to the terrorist attacks of September 11. Historically, however, big powers have always acted unilaterally. The United States did not ratify the Treaty of Versailles; France withdrew from the integrated military command of NATO; while China and France have repeatedly conducted nuclear tests despite strong protests from the international community.

5. It should not be ignored that, in the 10 years since the end of the cold war, Japanese public opinion has begun to move away from the main trends of the postwar era: fundamental opposition to any military action, and concern

only with peace for Japan. A survey, conducted immediately after the military action begun in Afghanistan by the United States, shows that 23 percent of the pollees considered this action "reasonable" and 60 percent "unavoidable," meaning that 83 percent either supported or could accept the U.S. intervention. Concerning Japan's role vis-à-vis Afghanistan, 63 percent favored support for the refugees. Presumably that support for U.S. actions has sharply declined since (*Yomiuri Shimbun* 23 October 2001).

6. According to a March 22, 2002, opinion poll conducted by the *Yomiuri Shimbun* newspaper of Diet members, half the respondents were in favor of the standing interpretations of the right to collective self-defense being revised.

BIBLIOGRAPHY

Baker III, James A., and Thomas M. DeFrank. 1995. *The Politics of Diplomacy: Revolution, War & Peace, 1989–1992.* New York: G.P. Putnam's Sons.

Bull, Hedley. 1995. *The Anarchical Society: A Study of Order in World Politics.* London: Macmillan.

Craig, Gordon A., and Alexander L. George. 1995. *Force and Statecraft.* New York: Oxford University Press.

Deutsch, Karl W., et al. 1975. *Political Community and the North Atlantic Area.* Princeton, N.J.: Princeton University Press.

Fujiwara Kiichi, ed. 2001a. *Tero-go: Sekai wa dō kawatta ka* (After the terrorist attacks: How has the world changed?). Tokyo: Iwanami Shoten.

———. 2001b. "Naisen to sensō no aida: Kokunai seiji to kokusai seiji no kyōkai ni tsuite" (Between war and civil war: A study of the borderline between domestic and international politics). In Japanese Political Science Association, ed. *Naisen wo meguru seijigakuteki kōsatsu: Nihon Seiji Gakkai nempō 2000.* (Politics of civil war: Annuals of the Japanese Political Science Association 2000). Tokyo: Iwanami Shoten.

Fukuyama, Francis. 1992. *The End of History and the Last Man.* New York: Free Press.

Hosoya Yūichi. 2001. "Amerika, dōmei, sekai chitsujo: Reisen-go Amerika ni okeru dōmei seisaku no hensen" (America, alliance, and world order: Changes in the U.S. policy toward alliance after the cold war). *Kokusai anzen hoshō* 29 (2).

Inoguchi Takashi. 2002. *Gendai Nihon seiji no kiso* (The base layers of contemporary Japanese politics). Tokyo: NTT Shuppan.

Iokibe Makoto, ed. 1999. *Sengo Nihon gaikōshi* (A history of postwar Japanese diplomacy). Tokyo: Yūhikaku.

Iwama Yōko. 1999. "Ōshū ni okeru kyōchōteki wakugumi no arikata: Kosobo kiki kara kangaeru (The framework for cooperation in Europe: Considering the Kosovo crisis). *Gaikō Forum* (November): 12–20.

Keddell, Jr. Joseph P. 1993. *The Politics of Defense in Japan: Managing Internal and External Pressures.* New York: M. E. Sharpe.

Kissinger, Henry. 2001. *Does America Need a Foreign Policy?: Toward a Diplomacy for the 21st Century.* New York: Simon & Schuster.

Kitaoka Shin'ichi. 1999. "Nihon no anzen hoshō: Reisengo jūnen no chiten kara" (Japan's security: Ten years after the cold war). *Gaikō Forum* (Special edition): 20–33.

———. 2002. "Dōji tahatsu tero to Nihon gaikō" (The terrorist attacks of September 11 and Japanese foreign policy). *Kokusai mondai* (March): 21–33.

Koseki Shōichi. 2001. *Kyūjō to anzen hoshō: "Heiwa to anzen" no saikentō* (Article 9 and security: Review of "peace and security"). Tokyo: Shōgakukan.

Miyazawa Kiichi. 2001. "Gekidō no hanseiki wo ikite" (Living through a half century of turbulence). *Kokusai mondai* (November): 50–79.

Mogami Toshiki. 2001. *Jindō-teki kainyū: Seigi no buryoku kōshi wa aru ka* (Humanitarian intervention: Is there any such thing as the "just" exercise of force?). Iwanami Shoten.

Murata Kōji. 2000. "Wakai sedai no kaiken-ron" (Constitution revision theories by the younger generations). *Chūō kōron* (June): 50–65.

Nakamura Akira. 2001. *Sengo seiji ni yureta kenpō kyūjō: Naikaku hōseikyoku no jishin to tsuyosa* (Article 9 of the constitution wavering in postwar politics: The Cabinet Legislation Bureau's self-confidence and strength). Tokyo: Chūō Keizaisha, second edition.

Nye, Joseph S. 1999. "Redefining the National Interest." *Foreign Affairs* 78 (4): 22–35.

Ōnuma Yasuaki. 1998. *Jinken, kokka, bunmei: Fuhen shugi-teki jinkenkan kara bunsai-teki jinkenkan e* (Human rights, the state, and civilization: From universal human rights to inter-civilization human rights). Tokyo: Chikuma Shobō.

Russett, Bruce. 1993. *Grasping the Democratic Peace: Principles for a Post-Cold War World.* Princeton, N.J.: Princeton University Press.

Sadakata Mamoru. 2000. "Kosobo funsō to NATO kūbaku" (The Kosovo war and NATO airstrikes). *Kokusai mondai* (June): 27–40.

Sakuma Hajime. 2002. "Ījisukan dasu beki datta" (Aejis ship should have been sent). *Yomiuri Shimbun* (10 March).

Sase Masamori. 2001. *Shūdanteki jieiken: Ronsū no tameni* (The right to collective self-defense: For debate). Tokyo: PHP Kenkyūsho.

Tanaka Akihiko. 1997. *Anzen hoshō: Sengo gojūnen no mosaku* (National security: Searching for ways over the fifty years since the war). Tokyo: Yomiuri Shimbun-sha.

———. 2000. *Wādo poroteikusu: Gurōbarīzeshon no naka no Nihon gaikō* (World politics: Japanese diplomacy in the era of globalization). Tokyo: Chikuma Shobō.

Yamazaki Masakazu. 1999."Insights into the World: Sovereignty Subjugated by Conscience." *Daily Yomiuri* (28 June).

———. 2001. "Bunmei shakai no chiteki taihai wo ureu: Terorizumu wa hanzai deshika nai" (Concern over intellectual decline in a civilized society: Terrorism is no more than a crime). *Chūō Kōron* (November): 32–42.

Yanai Shunji. 1999. "Nihon wa dō kōken dekiru ka" (How can Japan contribute?). *Gaikō Forum* (August): 28–32.

4. South Korea

Kim Sung-han

THE most fundamental pillar of international society is state sovereignty. This legal right ensures states' juridical equality, political independence, and territorial integrity. Thus, the norm of nonintervention is the corollary of state sovereignty, the latter not being possible without the former.

In the post–cold war era, however, a major threat to human rights in global society has come from quasi or failed states, that is, political communities in which government authority is weak or absent. Failed states generally result from two developments: a decline in the government's perceived legitimacy because of its unwillingness or inability to respond to popular demands, and the growing demands of ethnic, religious, and political minorities for increased political autonomy. These two developments have caused increased civil strife and a breakdown in government authority that has led to complex emergencies in numerous countries.

A complex emergency results from a confluence of internal conflicts, large-scale displacements of people, and fragile or failing economic, political, and social institutions. Other symptoms may include noncombatant deaths, starvation, or malnutrition; disease and mental illness; random and systematic violence against noncombatants; infrastructure collapse; widespread lawlessness; and interrupted food production and trade. The root causes of such emergencies are a combination of political power struggles, ethnic or religious tension, economic or territorial disputes, a perceived sense of widespread injustice, and/or natural disasters such as drought or flooding (Weiss and Collins 1996, 4).

Although the most flagrant violations of basic rights have historically occurred in oppressive dictatorial regimes, the most serious human rights abuses since the end of the cold war have stemmed from civil war and the breakdown of government authority. Thus, humanitarian intervention can be defined as foreign intervention—be it unilateral or multilateral—carried out to limit human suffering and death caused by government oppression or a country's political disintegration (Amstutz 1999, 136).

Humanitarian intervention can be distinguished from strategic intervention in that the latter seeks to advance the national interests of the intervening state. Some of the major goals pursued through strategic intervention include territorial security, regional stability, political interests, economic prosperity, and ideological interests. Examples of strategic intervention include the U.S. intervention in the Dominican Republic in 1965 and Grenada in 1983, both of which instances were aimed at preventing the spread of radical revolutionary regimes; and Vietnam's 1978 intervention in Cambodia and Tanzania's 1979 intervention in Uganda, in both of which cases the goal was to challenge repressive regimes that threatened territorial security and regional stability.[1]

The U.S.-led international military actions conducted during the cold war were mainly to contain the international expansion of communism. Internationalism was, in other words, the basis for an anticommunist movement. Humanitarian military actions since the end of the cold war can thus be seen as indicating a trend toward a new internationalism, because military force has been used—it is to be hoped after diplomatic efforts have all been exhausted—to contain crimes against humanity, thereby protecting human rights and democratic values around the globe. This new internationalism is now becoming the foundation for the human rights movement.

A shift is thus being made from negative, state-centered to positive, people-centered sovereignty. The 1990s saw human rights repeatedly trump sovereignty, with multiple invocations of Chapter VII of the Charter of the United Nations; the establishment of an International

Criminal Tribunal; criminal tribunals for Rwanda, Sierra Leone, and the former Yugoslavia; and Spanish efforts to extradite General Augusto Pinochet of Chile. During this period, on the one hand the UN Security Council manifestly broadened its interpretation of international peace and security to encompass human rights, humanitarian values, and even economic and social values that had previously been the sole purview of national governments, while on the other hand major world leaders showed greater willingness to go on the record as explicitly promoting the international prerogative that state sovereignty can be overridden in the face of gross violations of human rights or humanitarian law (Griffin 2000).

It is wrong to argue that universal human rights are an unprecedented challenge to sovereignty, since there has long been a struggle to establish international rules that compel leaders to treat their subjects in certain ways. Over the centuries, the emphasis has shifted from religious toleration, to minority rights (often focusing on particular ethnic groups in specific countries) and human rights (emphasizing the rights enjoyed by all or broad classes of individuals). After World War II, human rather than minority rights became the focus of attention, and the UN Charter endorses both human rights and the classic sovereignty principle of nonintervention (Krasner 2001, 22).

FROM NATIONAL TO HUMAN SECURITY

The growing international recognition of the human costs of conflict and other post–cold war developments have led the international community to reexamine the concept of security. Countries such as Australia, Canada, Sweden, Norway, and the Netherlands are at the forefront of this effort. A new concept of human security has emerged from this evolution in the form of the perception of international security. Human security recognizes that democratic development, human rights and fundamental freedoms, the rule of law, good governance, sustainable development, and social equity are as important to global peace as are arms control and disarmament.

In December 1996, it was agreed to at an Organization for Security and Co-operation in Europe (OSCE) summit that a comprehensive system of security for Europe must cover more than simply military security. It was also recognized that security includes the economic situation, social and environmental issues, human rights, as well as freedom of the press and media. Moreover, the final statement says, "The OSCE's comprehensive approach to security requires improvement in the implementation of all commitments in the human dimension, in particular with respect to human rights and fundamental freedoms. This will further anchor the common values of a free and democratic society in all participating States" (Organization for Security and Cooperation in Europe 1996).

Human security is thus much more than the absence of military threat. It includes security against economic privation, an acceptable quality of life, and a guarantee of fundamental human rights. At a minimum, human security requires that basic human needs be met, while acknowledging that sustained economic development, human rights and fundamental freedoms, the rule of law, good governance, sustainable development, and social equity are important to the achievement of lasting peace and stability (Axworthy 1997).

By mid-1997, all of Asia—with the exception of Cambodia, Laos, Myanmar, and North Korea—had become a showpiece of economic success, political stability, and, generally, social cohesion. However, Asia's economic confidence was suddenly undermined by an unexpected and explosive financial crisis that had a profound effect on the political and social solidarity of key Asian states. This period of economic stress aggravated conditions that precipitate human security transgressions. Human rights violations in East Asia, for instance, intensified, democratization was gagged, and threats to independent media increased. Electoral fraud, aggressive nationalism, racism, and involuntary migration all became more evident. Various areas in human security became paramount issues as the economic crisis came to dominate the region during the last years of the twentieth century.

HUMANITARIAN INTERVENTION:
LEGAL VERSUS MORAL PROBLEMS

Humanitarian intervention challenges the established international norm of state sovereignty and its corollary obligation of nonintervention. The claim that nonintervention is a morally valid norm in global society is based on several core assumptions and values, namely, that the existing anarchic international system is morally legitimate; people have a moral right to political self-determination; states have a juridical right to sovereignty and territorial integrity; states have an obligation to resolve conflicts peacefully; and force is an illegitimate instrument for altering existing territorial boundaries.

The most important legal prohibitions against intervention are contained in the UN Charter (Chapter 1, Article 2.4), which states that UN members are obligated to "refrain in their international relations from the threat or use of force against the territorial integrity or political independence of any state." Although nonintervention is the most basic constitutive norm of international society, states have historically intervened in the affairs of other states for a variety of reasons: a desire for economic expansion, the pursuit of strategic interests, a wish for territorial security, and humanitarian considerations. This is attributable to the oligarchic nature of international relations, which allows strong states to intervene in the domestic affairs of the weak (Guicherd 1999; Glennon 1999).

Ironically, the end of the cold war strengthened the oligarchic distribution of power in international relations and the United States remained the sole superpower. But it also deprived international relations of the U.S.-Soviet bipolar competition that had driven the two superpowers to intervene militarily in other states in order to increase their power and influence.

Another legal aspect of humanitarian intervention was highlighted by UN Secretary-General Kofi Annan. In his September 1999 address to the UN General Assembly, Annan expressed concern about the danger to the international order if states used force without the Security Council's authorization. But he tempered his concern by posing the following question: "If, in those dark days and hours leading up to the genocide [in Rwanda], a coalition of states had been prepared to act in defense of the Tutsi population, but did not receive prompt Council authorization, should such a coalition have stood aside and allowed the horror to unfold?" (United Nations 1999, 2). Annan's rhetorical question led member states to debate the merits of the doctrine of humanitarian intervention.

Morally, humanitarian intervention challenges the right of communal self-determination. Ethics is a discipline that deals with moral duty, and political thinkers have offered moral and legal arguments for the ethical legitimacy of sovereignty and nonintervention. Above all, the ethical challenge to peacekeepers is that their actions might be inimical to the interests of all the parties to the conflict despite the impartiality demanded of peacekeepers (Last 2000).

More serious moral problems, however, come to the fore when the international community does not respond to gross and systematic violations of human rights even after all diplomatic efforts have been exhausted. In other words, the doctrine of nonintervention carries with it the danger of omission—atrocities protected by the barrier of state sovereignty—while humanitarian intervention carries with it the danger of commission—either it is used as a cover or pretext for intervention for other motives, or the intervention is genuinely well-intentioned but does more harm than good. There is now a growing consensus supporting the moral claim that sovereignty is a contingent rather than an absolute value, the observance of which depends on a state upholding its responsibilities to protect the fundamental human rights and welfare of its citizens. There is a demonstrable difference in motives and results between intervention in support of this moral ground and the imperialism of yore (Tharoor and Daws 2001). Humanitarian intervention needs to be guided by principle if it is to win moral legitimacy from the international community.

Guiding Principles of Humanitarian Military Intervention

(Almost) the Last Resort   No state should attempt military intervention nor can it legitimately resort to war until all nonviolent alternatives, including diplomacy, multilateral negotiations, and sanctions have been exhausted.

A gross and systematic violation of human rights usually demands immediate response from the international community and thus needs to be managed realistically through the flexible application of the principle of last resort. Humanitarian military intervention can thus be attempted after the appropriate diplomatic efforts have been made, or even before they have all been exhausted.

Proportionality   Since the damage done by military action should be proportional to the good achieved by such an action, an indiscriminate war of attrition that seeks to eliminate the enemy society altogether is morally indefensible.

Humanitarian intervention must be in the interests of the people and communities of the state in which intervention has occurred; existing human rights violations must be reduced or eliminated and the preconditions for preventing their immediate recurrence established. Good intentions alone cannot justify humanitarian intervention.

Prospects for Success   A policy designed to relieve human suffering through military intervention must, if it is to be considered moral and humanitarian, have a high probability of successfully achieving its goals in both the short and medium terms. The prospects of success are thus closely linked to the so-called U.S. factor: humanitarian intervention that lacks U.S. commitment is not so likely to succeed.[2] The goals of humanitarian intervention are achieved when the United States perceives human rights abuses in a foreign country to be either a general threat to the order, legitimacy, and morality of global society or, as is most often the case, a threat to its own strategic interest in the region where the foreign country is located.

THE UNITED STATES
AND HUMANITARIAN MILITARY INTERVENTION
U.S. Military Intervention in the Post–Cold War Era

Although the cold war is over, military force remains the linchpin of U.S. foreign policy. During the last five or six years alone, the United States had bombed Iraq, an alleged pharmaceutical factory in Sudan, large areas of Serbia in a full-scale air war over Kosovo, and Afghanistan. In addition, the world's only superpower kept peace in Bosnia, occupied Haiti, and sent air and naval forces to the Taiwan Strait to show China just how committed the United States is to Taiwan.

Since the collapse of the Soviet Union and its conventional military power, the end of the Warsaw Pact, and Russia's adherence to arms control treaties, debate has raged over which U.S. interests—access to strategic resources and markets, keeping sea lanes open, the defense of the Korean peninsula and Japan, preventing/containing the proliferation of weapons of mass destruction (WMD), protecting allies and friendly states, and applying pressure on rogue states—can rightfully be considered vital. Although not usually described as such, the maintenance of the spirit of the Monroe Doctrine is also seen by Washington as a vital interest, given its various and frequent uses of military force in the western hemisphere during and after the cold war, despite the lack of a short- or long-term external threat. Today, some would stretch the definition of very important (if not absolutely vital) interests to include the promotion of basic U.S. values, particularly those of democracy and human rights, and humanitarian assistance.

A unipolar world has emerged since the disintegration of the Soviet Union, with the United States dominant in the military sphere. Compared to a bipolar system, military unipolarity places few constraints on the hegemon with regard to intervention in regional crises. What counts in the current unipolar era, in the absence of global rivalry and threat, is the relative importance of each specific region or subregion to the hegemon's interests, as well as the constraints on its military engagement there. The combined effects of interests and constraints can generate more specific and determinate expectations about the level of a great power's military engagement in regional crises (Miller 1998, 79).

Thus, the humanitarian crises in Kosovo and Rwanda received different levels of attention from the United States. The ethnic cleansing in Kosovo was defined as a humanitarian crisis by the United States and its allies, and thus saw U.S. military engagement; the United States recognized the geostrategic importance of Kosovo and felt less constrained in conducting military operations there due to its absolute air power. By contrast, the humanitarian situation in Rwanda did not induce a U.S. commitment, despite extensive CNN coverage, because Rwanda is outside Washington's geostrategic boundary. Clearly, these examples of U.S. liberalism on the offensive, or humanitarian military intervention, were the result of cool-headed strategic calculations.

Liberalism on the Offensive: Democratic Peace through U.S. Intervention

The core element of human security is human rights. One example of the trend to marry normative inquiries with strategic studies is the recently revived interest in the democratic peace proposition that democracies do not go to war against one another (Thakur 1997, 73). Justified by the democratic peace theory and a putative right to democracy, expectations are emerging at the multilateral, bilateral, and regional levels that a state desiring international legitimacy should clearly seek to democratize, and that external intervention to promote this is acceptable.[3]

Thus, an ideological base of humanitarian intervention is that democracies do not engage each other in war (Kant 1949). Democracies are far less likely to escalate disputes amongst themselves than are states that have other political systems (Maoz and Abdolali 1989). As the number of democracies increases, it is expected that the world will come closer to peace, for "the absence of war between democracies comes as close as anything we have to an empirical law in international relations" (Levy 1989, 88). This absence of war between democracies has come to be known as democratic peace. It is a bit early, however, to say that some of the humanitarian military intervention conducted since the end of the cold war has been successful in recovering or implanting democracy in the target states, even though gross and systematic violations of human rights may have ceased there.

The debate over democratic peace is important because it represents another round of the ongoing bout between realism and liberalism (Lynn-Jones 1996, ix). The existence of a democratic peace is usually seen as a liberal challenge to realist approaches to international relations. The apparent existence of a democratic peace calls into question two tenets common to most realist theory: realist pessimism about the prospects for international peace, and realist emphasis on systemic factors to explain international outcomes.

The U.S. promotion of democracy abroad, particularly as it has been pursued since the end of World War II, reflects a pragmatic, evolving, and sophisticated understanding of how to create a stable and relatively peaceful world order. It amounts to what might be called a liberal grand strategy, based on the realistic view that the political character of other states has an enormous impact on the ability of the United States to ensure its security and economic interests (Ikenberry 1999).

Since the end of the cold war, the liberal tendencies of U.S. strategy have gone on the offensive, as the United States has come to justify humanitarian military intervention as a way of promoting peace. During the cold war, the United States made every effort to defend liberal democracies and market economies against threats from the Soviet Union and the communist camp backing it. With the collapse of the Soviet Union, however, many in the United States concluded that democracy would spread across the globe and that world peace would soon be realized under Washington's leadership. By extension, were liberal democratic values to be threatened by any state, the United States and its allies would punish it. Thus, the United States' offensive liberalism has become the bedrock of humanitarian military intervention.

However, as should be obvious to observers, the United States talks out of both sides of its mouth. Reflecting the dislike of realpolitik, U.S. public discourse about foreign policy is usually couched in the language of liberalism. Hence, the pronouncements of policy elites are heavily flavored with optimism and moralism. Behind closed doors, however, the elites who formulate national security policy mostly speak the language of power, not of principles, and the United States acts according to the realist logic in the international arena. This gap between rhetoric and reality usually goes unnoticed because, at times, realist policies do coincide with the dictates of liberalism, on which occasions there is no conflict between the pursuit of power and principles. For example, the United States' fight against fascism during World War II and communism during the cold war was largely driven by realist reasons, while at the same time being consistent with liberal principles (Mearsheimer 2001, 26). Likewise, U.S. policymakers had little trouble selling to the public their 1999 military intervention in Kosovo as a liberal crusade to protect human rights.

Humanitarian Crusade: Kosovo

In March 1999, the North Atlantic Treaty Organisation (NATO) justified its use of force against Yugoslavia on the grounds that it was necessary to avert an impending humanitarian catastrophe. This action was very controversial because it was the first time since the founding of the United Nations that a group of states, acting without explicit UN Security Council authority, had defended a breach of the sovereignty rule primarily on humanitarian grounds.[4]

Commencing in February 1998, the conflict between the Kosovo Liberation Army (KLA) and the Yugoslav forces in Kosovo degenerated into a war of atrocities and ethnic cleansing. The fierce Serb offensive in the summer of 1998 left an estimated 1,500 Kosovar Albanians dead, while 300,000 fled their homes to hide in the mountains and forests. It could not be denied that a gross and systematic violation of human rights had been committed by the Yugoslav government.

The Serb atrocities in Kosovo led to the adoption of UN Security Council Resolution 1199 on September 23, 1998. They also led NATO to threaten air strikes in October, in order to force Belgrade to retreat from its extreme actions. The United States launched a diplomatic effort using mediation, which resulted in the agreement of October 15–18, 1998, brokered by the U.S. Balkans envoy Richard Holbrooke with President Slobodan Milosevic over the heads of ethnic Albanians and the KLA. The agreement brought a partial withdrawal of Serbian security forces and provided both for the deployment of up to 2,000 unarmed OSCE monitors in Kosovo and NATO-led aerial verification. Nevertheless, there was widespread skepticism as to whether the agreement would bring a lasting end to the mass murders and expulsions.

The killing on January 15, 1999, of at least 45 ethnic Albanians in the village of Racak, 29 kilometers southwest of the regional capital of Pristina, became a symbol of the breakdown of the October agreement. The Yugoslav authorities blocked numerous requests to allow investigators from the International Criminal Tribunal for the Former Yugoslavia to look into these and other killings, which led to a hardening of NATO member states' view that no political settlement for Kosovo would work unless it allowed for the deployment of a substantial NATO-led force. This further discouraged NATO from seeking UN Security Council approval for military action against Serbia. Questions concerning the NATO-pursued military means of securing proclaimed political and humanitarian ends were bound to elicit judgments on the legality of the operation. NATO's reliance on bombing gave rise to questions about its appropriateness, in terms of protecting the inhabitants of Kosovo, and its conformity with the laws of war (Roberts 1999, 108).

Thus it is hard to say that the NATO air strikes were conducted as a last resort per se. The United States and a group of democratic countries in Europe had launched a humanitarian crusade to correct the inhumane situation in Kosovo, and NATO's allied force launched an air strike against Yugoslavia, diplomatic efforts having failed. However, the air strike generated international controversy because the military action had bypassed the UN Security Council.

The conduct of war is traditionally assumed to be ruled by two principles: discrimination and proportionality. Under the first principle, it is unethical to target noncombatants, although it is acknowledged that they may be killed as an unintended result of attacks on military targets. The principle of proportionality, however, limits the acceptability of collateral damage. The war in Yugoslavia was not one in which two sides fought each other but, rather, a one-sided process in which NATO rained bombs on Yugoslavia from the skies while refusing to come close on the ground lest its forces be endangered. A pilot bombing a target from 4,600 meters above the ground never sees his enemy, does not have to fight him, and thus sees no need to honor him or behave with restraint toward him (Robinson 1999). The emphasis on airpower in this campaign, coupled with the U.S. reluctance to risk the lives of its servicemen, exposed certain problems about the extent to which NATO was able to perform its military tasks effectively and minimize civilian damage.

Lastly, one must ask whether the humanitarian military intervention was successful. Despite the fine line between success and failure, NATO's intervention did stop the gross and systematic violations of human rights in Kosovo, a success mainly attributable to U.S. commitment. Two months into the bombing campaign, there were looming prospects that is might have to continue over the summer. To the relief of NATO governments, on June 3, Milosevic formally accepted the joint European Union–Russian peace terms that had been presented to him the previous day. This led to the military agreement signed at Kumanovo air base in Macedonia on June 9, and to UN Security Council Resolution 1244 the following day. Air power, mainly that of the United States, played a significant role; had the military operation been conducted without U.S. participation, Milosevic would not have stopped. Even before the air strikes, the prospects for the success of the humanitarian intervention in Kosovo had been high, because the United States was considered a decisive NATO participant. In addition, the reality that there could be, and the threat of, land operations also played a part. On May 31, the U.S. government gave General Wesley

Clark permission to strengthen and widen the road in Albania that led from the port of Durres to Kukes on the Kosovo border. This was a way of conveying to Milosevic the fact that invasion was a serious option.[5]

Intervention in East Timor: U.S. Inaction

The situation surrounding East Timor was unfinished business remaining from the colonial era. Shortly after Portugal granted independence to East Timor, Indonesia in 1975 moved to annex, by brute force, the new state in aggression that resembled Iraq's attack on Kuwait (Falk 1999, 374). The geopolitical climate of the cold war had encouraged a wink and a nod at Indonesia's aggression. But with the end of the cold war, as moves to gain independence by the East Timorese provoked bloody repression by Indonesia of a horrifying magnitude, this changed: Jakarta was no longer seen as a vital ally.

Intervention in Kosovo was an anomaly, but the case of East Timor reaffirmed the long-accepted international rules of intervention. The September 1999 activities of the International Force in East Timor (INTERFET) had the formal consent of Indonesia and East Timor, as well as UN Security Council authorization. There was also a strong moral rationale for intervention, because East Timor had seen persistent human rights violations with approximately 120,000 to 200,000 East Timorese having been killed since 1975 (Emmerson 1999/2000). In response to the Indonesian state-sponsored terror, a combination of the United States' geopolitical pressure on the government in Jakarta, Australia's regional responsibility to supply most of the personnel for a peacekeeping mission, and a formal UN mandate provided some relief for the East Timorese.

Australia, Thailand, and South Korea led the military operation in East Timor, while big powers, including China, provided political support. This was done so that the big powers could avoid giving the impression that they were seeking to exert neocolonial influence on East Timor. The case of East Timor can be viewed as an ideal model for future humanitarian intervention as it met all the criteria for legitimate humanitarian intervention. But it was an exceptional case, because there were no disagreements among the major powers, and East Timor is located outside the geostrategic focal point of the big powers.

SOUTH KOREA'S EMERGING PERSPECTIVE

Coalition Among Like-Minded Countries

The following two statements, one by a foreign minister and the other by a former ambassador to Geneva, highlight South Korea's commitment to human rights.

> Without security and economic development, human rights cannot be genuine. Democracy and human rights cannot flourish without a certain degree of economic prosperity. . . . In dealing with this problem, we should bear in mind that a simplistic and self-righteous approach to the issue of human rights could be counter-productive by provoking another powerful human sentiment, namely, nationalism. Compassion and pragmatism, rather than subjective moralism, should be our guiding principle. (Han 1993)

> Korea is concerned with the systematic violation of human rights occurring on a large scale in those areas embroiled in civil wars and conflicts. It rests with the members of the international community to cooperate closely with each other and take effective steps to prevent such large-scale human rights violations. The construction of efficient early-warning systems and, most importantly, the implementation of measures to prevent conflict are called for. Moreover, efforts must be exerted to eradicate the culture of impunity around the world. As the situation in Kosovo and East Timor illustrated, the causes of systematic and massive human rights violations are rooted in discrimination and prejudice against different races and religions. We believe that the lofty spirit and principles enshrined in the Universal Declaration of Human Rights can be materialized when a culture of tolerance prevails among different races, religions, and cultures. (Chang 2000)

South Korea has for some time been an active participant in international discussions on human rights. Thus, for example, at the fifty-sixth session of the Commission on Human Rights held in Geneva on March 29, 2000, South Korea participated in adopting the Australia-initiated resolution on human rights and good governance as a joint sponsor together with Chile, South Africa, and Poland. Moreover,

South Korea has been trying to expand its diplomatic horizon by paying growing attention to human security issues, particularly in Asia Pacific. But such issues do not just require interest: They necessitate knowledge.

If these issues are to be appropriately addressed, the security experts in the region should form an epistemic community, since human security encompasses a wide array of complex issues—political and socioeconomic insecurity; intrastate ethnic conflict and involuntary migration; drug trafficking and transnational crime; and environmental degradation—that are interconnected and thus require that policymakers have broad-based knowledge and information if they are to identify their state interests and recognize the latitude of action deemed appropriate in specific issue areas of human security. Control of knowledge and information is an important dimension of power, and the diffusion of new ideas and information can both lead to new patterns of behavior and be an important determinant of international policy coordination (Kim 2000, 295).

An epistemic community is a network of professionals with recognized expertise and competence in a particular domain, and an authoritative epistemic community may comprise professionals from a variety of disciplines and backgrounds (Haas 1992, 2–3). The Council for Security Cooperation in the Asia Pacific (CSCAP) is an example of such a network.

Were epistemic communities on human security to help define the self-interests of a state, like-minded countries could build a coalition. Certainly not a few countries would realize that power is to be obtained from networking and coalition-building, while government officials will probably try to establish issue-based coalitions with other countries in various fields of human security.

Such coalitions would function best were they to identify and collaborate on specific functions and tasks. The rapid exchange of information could strengthen activities such as the addressing of human rights abuses and international crime, in which areas a timely exchange of information across borders is essential. Inter-regional epistemic communities could also establish free media and counter hate propaganda, thereby bolstering democracy and reducing the likelihood of conflict in troubled areas. At the moment, democratic front-runners such as the United States, Japan, Australia, Canada, New Zealand, and

South Korea have the best chance of forging coalitions to tackle human security issues.

Preventing Humanitarian Tragedies

Punishment through humanitarian military intervention alone cannot reduce the rate of crimes against humanity. This must be supplemented by preventive diplomacy aimed at improving human security if humanitarian tragedies are to be prevented. Human rights and regional security issues are inextricably linked, the security of nation states resting on the security of those states' civil societies. The security problems that beset Asia Pacific—notably in Cambodia, North Korea, East Timor, and Myanmar—in fact reflect human rights violations, which are the root cause of regional security issues that preclude the resolution of conflicts, confidence building, and the strengthening of multilateral cooperation (Mungoven 1997). Thus, the violation of human rights must be prevented.

As former UN Secretary-General Boutros Boutros-Ghali aptly stated, preventive diplomacy is an "action to prevent disputes from arising between parties, to prevent existing disputes from escalating into conflicts, and to limit the spread of the latter when they occur" (Boutros-Ghali 1992, 5).[6] With respect to implementation and practical modalities, there are several operational measures whereby preventive diplomacy can be conducted: confidence building, fact finding, early warning, the creation of demilitarized zones, preventive deployment, and preventive diplomatic measures—which would include institution building and preventive humanitarian action.

Preventive diplomacy has acquired new meaning since the emergence of the concept of cooperative security, which has replaced the cold-war concept of collective security (Nolan et al. 1994, 5–6). Interest is growing in nontraditional security threats, such as economic conflict, population movements, narcotics, transnational environmental problems, and religious and ethnic nationalism. If these threats cannot be effectively met with traditional forms of readiness and deterrence, more constructive and sophisticated forms of influence and intervention are required in the form of cooperative security. By the same token, the guarantee of human security rests on the implementation of the fundamental measures of preventive diplomacy.

Should Regional Organizations Take the Lead?

There is a growing sentiment within the United Nations that regional organizations should be active—and perhaps even take the lead—in preventing and resolving humanitarian crises. Perhaps the ASEAN Regional Forum (ARF) could develop its own set of criteria to determine when it should become involved in intervention activities.

ARF is one of the few multilateral security regimes that have emerged recently outside Europe. Not a multilateral institution but a multilateral organization,[7] ARF sees itself as a body that can discuss and solve conflicts in Southeast Asia, Northeast Asia, and Oceania. ARF foresees that its role will gradually evolve in three stages, namely, the promotion of confidence-building measures, the development of preventive diplomacy mechanisms, and the development of conflict-resolution mechanisms.

While this evolutionary scheme might appear somewhat idealistic, it might be realistic, for example, to find ways for ARF to reach the second stage earlier than expected. Although ARF may still be far from an institution for conflict resolution able to resolve humanitarian crises, it could well take a step forward toward becoming an organization of conflict prevention.[8]

In the meantime, ARF member states need to consolidate their regional identity, since this, together with the perception of close geographical proximity, can also provide an impetus for humanitarian intervention. In the case of East Timor, the sense of regional identity helped override strong presumptions against intervention, and made it difficult for ASEAN states to ignore events occurring in their own backyard. Perceived proximity can lend strong support for and understanding of the need to take action, while failure to take action could be interpreted as a sign of impotence. Thus, with good reason, ASEAN states may have felt little reluctance to act (Singapore Institute of International Affairs 2001, 13).

However, ASEAN failed to act as a unified body on East Timor's behalf, Thailand having participated in the international peacekeeping force with Australia and South Korea. ARF also failed to act, possibly because a sense of regional identity was wanting. In light of the less optimistic prospects for ARF as a multilateral institution for conflict resolution, humanitarian intervention might be expected from U.S. allies, such as South Korea, Japan, and Australia, which would increase the likelihood that humanitarian military interventions would succeed.

HUMANITARIAN INTERVENTION
DESPITE SEPTEMBER 11

To intervene or not to intervene? This is the question that has tormented foreign ministries and defense establishments of the major powers since the end of the cold war. Humanitarian intervention during the cold war was a cause that dared not speak its name.

All that has changed. It is not only that the goalposts have shifted, and that national frontiers—and what governments do within them —are no longer sacrosanct, but that no one can quite locate the goalposts. Intervention that now tends to be multilateral rather than unilateral, as during the cold war, is that much more complicated and problematic to undertake and sustain.

Rather than go down the road of championing the right of interference and the codification of humanitarian intervention as changes to the UN Charter, we should gradually build a new body of international law and practice. Such a very Anglo-Saxon, common law approach has its defects, but it must surely be the only way that the recent changes in dealing with humanitarian emergencies can be consolidated and pursued. Even a degree of uncertainty can have a deterrent effect.

In the end, however, the real problems surrounding humanitarian intervention are not legal or conceptual: They are severely practical. The real question is, thus, will those with the capability to intervene have the will to do so? Will nations be prepared to risk their soldiers' lives and incur heavy costs in faraway countries about which their electorates know little? On that, the jury is still out, and it is wise for even the most enthusiastic advocates of intervention to temper their advocacy with a little realism, which is not a synonym for realpolitik.

While it does not take an Einstein of diplomacy to predict that the international community will soon be faced with other examples of supreme humanitarian emergencies, it is a lot less easy to predict how it will react to them. Much will, of course, depend on the administration of U.S. President George W. Bush. Soon enough, it will be judged not by what its individual members may have said when they held positions of authority in the 1990s, but by what they do when confronted with a real live crisis in the new century.

If the twenty-first century is to represent progress from the twentieth century, then surely a key yardstick for judging this progress will be whether the international community is better able to prevent humanitarian emergencies, and deal with them should they occur.

Since the September 11 terrorist attacks, the United States has been preoccupied with the war against terrorism, for which reason it will not in the foreseeable future intervene in humanitarian tragedies unless they have a link to terrorism. Realistically, a decline in the U.S. commitment to combating humanitarian catastrophes might mean the end of humanitarian intervention.

Certainly it would be dangerous for the United States to focus solely on its antiterrorism war to the exclusion of other potentially lethal dangers. The question of North Korea should not be forgotten. Bad weather on the Korean peninsula could lead to a much more devastating storm than that in Afghanistan. Unless a strong, well-financed, and long-term nation-building effort is made in the Balkans by the United States and Europe, we will face the unraveling of a fragile peace over the coming years.

The United States, while conducting a war against terrorism, also needs to lead international efforts to prevent humanitarian tragedies. It should focus on diplomacy to prevent disputes from arising between parties and existing disputes from escalating into conflicts, and to limit the spread of disputes when they occur. Moreover, the United States should take care to ensure that human rights are not abused in the name of counter-terrorism if there is to be a durable, long-term approach whereby humanity can prevail over terrorism.

NOTES

1. Some experts argue that the Vietnamese intervention in Cambodia in December 1978 was conducted on humanitarian grounds, since it ended Pol Pot's reign of terror. Stephen A. Garrett (1999), for example, puts more weight on the humanitarian outcome of the Vietnamese action than on the humanitarian motives, arguing that the intervention was genuinely humanitarian despite the lack of any humanitarian rationale. However, the primacy of humanitarian motives should be established as a litmus test. This does not

preclude mixed motives, but it would disqualify those interventions that, lacking a humanitarian motive, nevertheless produce a humanitarian outcome. While the results of the Vietnamese intervention was the rescue of the Cambodian people from a catastrophic human rights situation, humanitarian reasons appear to have played no part in the decision to intervene, as can be understood from Foreign Minister Nguyen Co Thach's comment to U.S. Congressman Steven Solarz that "human rights was not a question; that was their problem . . . We were concerned only with security" (Wheeler 2001).

2. In terms of humanitarian military intervention, the distinction must be drawn between a UN force and a UN-authorized force. In the event that the Security Council exercises operational command and control over a force, it is considered to be a UN force, as in the case of a UN peacekeeping force (UNPKF). However, if operational command and control is exercised by either a member state or a regional organization, the body is a UN-authorized force. An international peacekeeping force (IPF) (UN-authorized force) is usually preferable to a UNPKF (UN force) because it is quicker to respond to humanitarian crises, as was seen in the case of the Bosnian crisis. Once an emergency has been defused, an IPF can be replaced by a UNPKF, as was recently done in East Timor.

3. Gow (2000) has interpreted this as the "internationalization" of sovereignty, whereby a state is judged on "the degree to which it is a net contributor to systemic and societal stability."

4. China expressed three objections. First, it opposed the internationalization of domestic affairs, and so was against foreign involvement in domestic ethnic disputes, even for humanitarian reasons. Second, the United Nations had been bypassed; NATO had dismissed UN authority to decide what constituted a threat to international peace and stability, and when humanitarian intervention should be undertaken. Third, military force had been employed to advance these goals (Gill and Reilly 2000, 47).

5. The argument that air power was really effective in Kosovo is, however, controversial. Air power has punitive uses and perhaps even coercive utility if the pain inflicted is sufficiently great. In Kosovo, however, it did not prevent the murders and forced expulsions that were NATO's justification for intervention (Daadler and O'Hanlon 1999).

6. Boutros-Ghali made an excellent attempt at defining, both as a concept and as an activity, preventive diplomacy, which had remained largely undefined since the end of the cold war. During the cold war, the goal of preventive diplomacy had simply been to keep local conflicts from becoming entangled in superpower rivalry—in other words, to keep new conflicts outside the sphere of inter-bloc differences.

7. While multilateral organizations are a quantitative concept, highlighting the number of participants, the concept of multilateral institutions is a qualitative one, referring to a situation in which state behavior in a group of

more than three states is characterized by the following three elements: 1) the indivisibility of welfare; 2) the nondiscriminatory or equal application of some generalized principles; and 3) diffuse reciprocity. The first element exists when member states make no clear distinction between their individual interests and those of the group as a whole. The second element applies when a particular member state engages in an act for another member state in order to achieve a goal of their multilateral organization; there is no discrimination among states and the same behavioral code applies to every state. The third element is seen in such situations as when member states reciprocate cooperative behavior without requesting specific rewards or compensation, such as reciprocity based on the expectation of others' good will. In light of this rigorous delineation of concepts, ARF is still far from being a multilateral institution, because each member state, which has agreed neither on a common behavioral code nor on loose reciprocity, acts in its own national interests rather than those of ARF (Ruggie 1993).

8. ARF identifies several activities as constituting preventive diplomacy. These include using good offices to resolve conflicts, third-party mediation, conducting fact-finding, and moral persuasion (ASEAN Regional Forum Working Group on Preventive Diplomacy 1996).

BIBLIOGRAPHY

Amstutz, Mark R. 1999. *International Ethics: Concepts, Theories, and Cases in Global Politics.* Lanham: Rowman and Littlefield.

ASEAN Regional Forum Working Group on Preventive Diplomacy. 1996. "Chairman's Statement." <http://www.aseansec.org/print.asp?file=/politics/arf4xh.htm> (22 October 2002).

Axworthy, Lloyd. 1997. "Canada and Human Security: the Need for Leadership." *International Journal* 52(2): 183–196.

Boutros-Ghali, Boutros. 1992. "An Agenda for Peace: Preventive Diplomacy, Peace-Making and Peace-Keeping." Report of the Secretary-General pursuant to the statement adopted by the Summit Meeting of the Security Council on 31 January 1992. <http://www.un.org/docs/sg/agpeace.html> (28 November 2002).

Chang Man-Soon. 2000. Address to the 56th Session of the Commission on Human Rights. Geneva, 29 March.

Daadler, Ivo H., and Michael O'Hanlon. 1999. "Unlearning the Lessons of Kosovo." *Foreign Policy* 116(Fall): 128–140.

Emmerson, Donald K. 1999/2000. "Moralpolitik: The Timor Test." *The National Interest* (Winter): 63–68.

Falk, Richard. 1999. "The New Interventionism and the Third World." *Current History* (November).

Garrett, Stephen A. 1999. *Doing Good and Doing Well: An Examination of Humanitarian Intervention.* Westport, Conn.: Praeger.

Gill, Bates, and James Reilly. 2000. "Sovereignty, Intervention and Peacekeeping: The View from Beijing." *Survival* 42(3) Autumn: 41–59.

Glennon, Michael F. 1999. "The New Interventionism: The Search for a Just International Law." *Foreign Affairs* 78(3): 2–7.

Gow, James. 2000. "A Revolution in International Affairs?" *Security Dialogue* 31(3): 293–306.

Griffin, Michele. 2000. "Where Angels Fear to Tread: Trends in International Intervention" *Security Dialogue* 31(4): 424–425.

Guicherd, Catherine. 1999. "International Law and the War in Kosovo." *Survival* 4(2): 19–34.

Haas, Peter M. 1992. "Introduction: Epistemic Communities and International Policy Coordination." *International Organization* 46(1).

Han Sung-joo. 1993. "New World Order and Human Rights." Statement at the World Conference on Human Rights Vienna, 15 June.

Ikenberry, G. John. 1999. "Why Export Democracy?: The 'Hidden Grand Strategy' of American Foreign Policy." *The Wilson Quarterly* 23(2). <http://www.mtholyoke.edu/acad/intrel/exdem.htm>.

Kant, Immanuel. 1949. "Eternal Peace." In Carl Friedrich ed. *The Philosophy of Kant.* New York: Random House.

Kim Sung-han. 2000. "Human Security and Regional Cooperation: Preparing for the Twenty-First Century." In William T. Tow, Ramesh Thakur, and In Taek Hyun. *Asia's Emerging Regional Order: Reconciling Traditional and Human Security.* Tokyo: United Nations University Press.

Krasner, Stephen D. 2001. "Sovereignty." *Foreign Policy* 122(January/February): 20–29.

Last, Major D. M. 2000. "Reflections from the Field: Ethical Challenges in Peacekeeping and Humanitarian Interventions." *The Fletcher Forum of World Affairs* (Spring): 73–86.

Levy, Jack S. 1989. "Domestic Politics and War." In Robert I. Rotberg and Theodore K. Rabb, eds. *The Origin and Prevention of Major Wars.* Cambridge, U.K.: Cambridge University Press.

Lynn-Jones, Sean M. 1996. "Preface." In Michael E. Brown, Sean M. Lynn-Jones, and Steven E. Miller, eds. *Debating the Democratic Peace.* Cambridge, Mass.: The MIT Press.

Maoz, Zeeve, and Nasrin Abdolali. 1989. "Regime Types and International Conflict." *Journal of Conflict Resolution* 33(1): 3–35.

Mearsheimer, John J. 2001. *The Tragedy of Great Power Politics.* New York: W. W. Norton & Company.

Miller, Benjamin. 1998. "The Logic of US Military Interventions in the Post–Cold War Era." *Contemporary Security Policy* 19(3).

Mungoven, Rory. 1997. "Human Rights and Regional Security: A Challenge for the ASEAN Regional Forum." <http://web.amnesty.org/ai.nsf/Index/IOR640011997?OpenDocument&of=COUNTRIES%5CCAMBODIA> (22 October 2002).

Nolan, Janne E. et al. 1994. "The Concept of Cooperative Security." In Janne E. Nolan ed. *Global Engagement: Cooperation & Security in the 21st Century*. Washington, D.C.: The Brookings Institution.

Organization for Security and Co-operation in Europe. 1996. "Lisbon Document." <http://www.osce.org/docs/english/1990-1999/summits/lisbo96e.htm> (10 Ocober 2002).

Roberts, Adam. 1999. "NATO's 'Humanitarian War' over Kosovo." *Survival* 41(3): 102–123.

Robinson, Paul. 1999. "Ready to Kill But Not to Die: NATO Strategy in Kosovo." *International Journal* (Autumn).

Ruggie, John Gerald. 1993. "Multilateralism: The Anatomy of an Institution." In John Gerald Ruggie, ed. *Multilateralism Matters: The Theory and Praxis of an Institutional Form*. New York: Columbia University Press.

Singapore Institute of International Affairs. 2001. "Sovereignty and Intervention." Special Report.

Thakur, Ramesh. 1997. "From National to Human Security." In Stuart Harris and Andrew Mack, eds. *Asia-Pacific Security: The Economics-Politics Nexus*. St. Leonards, Australia: Allen and Unwin.

Tharoor, Sashi, and Sam Daws. 2001. "Humanitarian Intervention: Getting Past the Reefs." *World Policy Journal* (Summer): 22–27.

United Nations. 1999. Secretary General's Annual Report to the General Assembly. Press Release SG/SM7136 GA/9596, September 20.

Weiss, Thomas G., and Cindy Collins. 1996. *Humanitarian Challenges and Intervention: World Politics and the Dilemmas of Help*. Boulder, Colo.: Westview Press.

Wheeler, Nicholas J. 2001. "Humanitarian Intervention after Kosovo: Emergent Norm, Moral Duty or the Coming Anarchy?" *International Affairs* 77(1): 113–128.

5. India

Jasjit Singh

THE concept that sovereignty rests with the state, which is sovereign within its boundaries, has long been a source of tension. The principle of sovereignty was inherited from the rights of the sovereign king, and codified relations between the ruler and the ruled on one side, and among states on the other. The American and French revolutions modified this state order, shifting it from being largely a charter of the rulers to that, shaped by the new social contract between the rulers and the ruled, which emerged from the socio-political changes in the wake of the Industrial Revolution.

The three revolutions sanctified the equality of human beings and enshrined the notion of citizenship of the state. There thus emerged the idea of state sovereignty within borders and the principle of nonintervention by one state in the internal affairs of the other. At the same time, however, the Industrial Revolution provided the means and impetus for the rapid spread of colonial empires, which resulted in the regression of industry and shrinking of the economic base of productivity in countries such as India and China. It thereby increased the gap between the imperial sovereign states and the colonized countries.

As a result of the tension that has arisen while the principles associated with sovereignty have evolved, numerous norms, conventions, and legal treaties have been fashioned over the centuries to modulate and manage the use of force both within a state—by the rule of law and often defined by a constitution—as well as between states. But in recent years, the central logic of state sovereignty and nonintervention has come to be questioned, in the context of humanitarian intervention, particularly regarding the issue of human rights violations.

SOVEREIGNTY IN THE
TWENTY-FIRST CENTURY

It is ironic that as states acquired independence and, hence, sovereignty, during the last half of the twentieth century, the concept of sovereignty was increasingly questioned in developed countries. Some would explain this simply as the questioning of the established order, since the concept of a modern democratic state when applied at the international level would require empowerment of developing, weak, small states. Following two bitterly fought, long and debilitating wars that had sucked in countries and people across the world, others saw the coming together of sovereign states of western Europe as marking the start of the sovereign state's decline. While it can be argued that the issue of sovereignty and the need to subdue it has often been used as a foreign policy tool and that the selective use of concepts like self-determination, human rights, and intervention have been pursued by some with ideological or politico-strategic goals, objective analysis reveals that questions related to the future of sovereignty need to be addressed. But before examining the political and strategic dimensions of sovereignty and its relationship to the use of force in intervention, a number of basic issues should be noted.

The Sovereign State: The Basic Norm

The concept of sovereignty has existed throughout most of history. The sovereign state (and, in the ideal state, the sovereignty that it exercises on behalf of its people) continues to be the basic norm, the only constitutional institution to confer power on a group of citizens to function in the modern world, and the cornerstone of international relations as well as domestic governance. Sovereignty, therefore, "strictly speaking, is a legal institution that authenticates a political order based on independent states whose governments are the principal authorities both domestically and internationally" (Jackson 1999, 10).

Sovereign states of the world have joined the United Nations which, in 1945 adopted a charter to provide the legal and political framework to direct the management of international relations between the sovereign states; Chapter I, Article 2 (1) of the Charter of the United Nations categorically states that "The Organization is based on the principle of the sovereign equality of all its Members." The United Nations, as an organization of sovereign nation-states with a defined charter, would lose its raison d'être and be irreparably weakened were the principle of sovereignty not sustained in letter and spirit. This was seen during the 1999 North Atlantic Treaty Organisation (NATO) intervention in Kosovo. Moreover, the concept of sovereignty would, in turn, be severely undermined were one sovereign state to violate internationally accepted norms, its treaty obligations, and/or the UN Charter by committing acts of aggression against another. This was seen when Iraq invaded Kuwait in 1990, and in the case of Pakistan's aggression against India in 1999.

A large number of modern states have adopted a constitution according to which they seek to govern the society they encompass. This constitution replaces the person of the sovereign ruler, and provides the ideological, legal, and political framework within which the state is to function. Hence fundamental rights, the rule of law, the consultative process, social justice, territorial boundaries, and a host of aspirations of the people and their commitments are transcribed into the constitution that thus becomes the symbol and substance of sovereignty.

It is important to note that there is as yet no viable alternative to the system of sovereign state, notwithstanding suggestions that the European Union represents the emerging model of a changed Westphalian system. It should not be forgotten that the fifteen state members of the European Union exercised their sovereignty to take the decision to establish and join the union, none of them having given up their national sovereignty.

Limited Parameters

Sovereignty was never absolute. This is not to suggest that kings and states have not attempted to practice absolutism, but objective factors inevitably placed limits on the extent of sovereignty that could be exercised. The concept of sovereignty is not negated although in practice the sovereignty of the weaker ruler or state may get eroded or even trampled upon. In essence, the degree of sovereignty even in domestic affairs is conditioned by what has often been defined as the social contract between the ruler and the ruled.

In ancient India, this concept was enshrined in the principle that the king has obligations toward his subjects; a *dharma* (duty), if not fulfilled by the ruler, gave his subjects legitimacy to act against him. This social contract is well established in modern democratic states on the basis of both accountability and the legitimacy of the rulers. Usurpation of democracy brings into question the legitimacy of the ruler, although it does not alter the fundamental sovereignty of the country.

A Conflictual Model

There is no denying that the sovereign-state system has not provided a less conflictual model than the pre-Westphalian framework. But increasingly serious efforts have been made to manage the difficulties arising out of international relations among independent countries as the instrumentalities of war and destruction have increased in range, complexity, and lethality. This has been seen with the establishment of the League of Nations and, later, the United Nations. While some countries are more powerful and have additional rights, the United Nations continues to be an organization of sovereign states and its charter emphasizes the principle of sovereign equality, non-interference in the affairs of other sovereign states, and the non-use of threats against sovereign states.

Terminal Decline

The conventional wisdom of some would have one believe that, as we move into the twenty-first century, the heretofore accepted concept of sovereignty is in a state of terminal decline, which, according to some, would legitimize intervention in the internal affairs of other countries. Three propositions are usually advanced to support the view that sovereignty is declining: First, globalization is rendering sovereignty an obsolescent concept; second, multinational companies, nongovernmental organizations, and nonstate actors—in a world dominated by networking and the information revolution—are eroding national sovereignty; and third, increasing interdependence in trade as well as economic and financial relations, together with environmental concerns, signify increasing internationalization at the cost of national sovereignty.

Globalization certainly is intruding into many segments of a state's functions. The information revolution has deeply intruded into not only the domestic arena of sovereign states, but also the cultural and personal life of the people in states. Multinational companies are operating across frontiers of sovereign states giving rise to apprehensions of loss of sovereignty at least in the economic-industrial field. International finance and trading systems deeply affect the economies of countries across the globe, as has been demonstrated by the events leading to the East Asian economic crisis and surrounding Black Tuesday (September 11, 2001), when terrorist attacks on the United States caused the New York Stock Exchange to be closed. Yet, the core decisions regarding globalization are the result of the exercise of sovereign decisions by states.

While globalization might define the terms and conditions according to which sovereign states interact in economic and trade/technology terms—as the World Trade Organization (WTO) mostly does—becoming part of the process depends on a state making the decision to do so by exercising its sovereign right. It would seem that sovereignty thus will remain the key principle in interstate relations.

The future of the sovereign state, however, is governed by the international system. As new centers of power have emerged over the past two decades or so, the world order has become polycentric, which has required that the principle of sovereignty be strengthened rather than weakened.

UNEQUAL SOVEREIGN STATES

A major source of tension is the fact that, while in principle, all states are equal and sovereign, in reality they are endowed with unequal capabilities and assets for reasons of geography and history. Many of the weaker states have emerged as a result of the desire and struggle of small groups within a large plural entity to set up a sovereign state. The former Federal Republic of Yugoslavia is the most recent example, while the creation of Pakistan and Bangladesh, which resulted in the breakup of India in 1947 and Pakistan in 1971, are examples of the unwillingness or inability of some to accept the principle that all human beings are equal and to manage majority-minority relations in an equitable manner.

The evolution of the sovereign nation-state has not been uniform worldwide, however. The states of the South transited from monarchy-based sovereignty in the precolonial period to a denial of sovereignty during the colonial interregnum, when the western European model of the sovereign state was finding its roots in metropolitan states. The state building process was profoundly impacted by four characteristics of the colonial period, namely, arbitrary boundaries; the promotion of multiple authorities in colonized states; de-industrialization and nonindustrialization; and rapid decolonization, which did not allow enough time for states to function as modern sovereign entities on the foundations of what in the West had emerged from the American and French revolutions.

As a consequence, the level of development of the modern state, liberal democratic institutions and culture, human rights, attitudes to the use of force, and perceived national/strategic interests are different in the countries of western Europe and in developing countries, as well as among the states in the developing world. It is against this background that one must understand the clash of civilizations on one hand, and on the other the difficulties involved in arriving at an acceptable framework for intervention in support of human rights in a state.

There is a view that external intervention—especially humanitarian intervention by the international community—is required in many cases, and that this can only be undertaken by subsuming the principle of sovereignty. This approach totally ignores the basic reasons for which humanitarian violations originally take place.

Developing countries are now in the process of nation-state building—much like the developed countries during the eighteenth and nineteenth centuries. Emerging from centuries of denial of freedom, they are naturally sensitive to the principle of sovereign equality, which must be sustained if nation-state building is to be pursued in any meaningful way.

It is the faltering of the nation-state building process which leads to circumstances that worsen the mostly fragile humanitarian conditions in the developing world. Rwanda, Angola, Somalia, Afghanistan, and a host of examples are testimony to this phenomenon. The needs of humanitarian intervention must be met with assistance aimed at building the nation-state, rather than military intervention in its name.

INTERVENTION IN A WORLD OF SOVEREIGN STATES

The term intervention has broad interpretations, ranging from intervention by political, economic, and diplomatic means to intervention with the use of force, traditionally seen in terms of military force. But lately, intervention has been taking place with the use of force employing unconventional means and methods, thereby further complicating the issues.

Proscription by the UN Charter

By definition, intervention implies the use of force by a state or organization/entity inside another sovereign state without the latter's concurrence, and in violation of the sovereignty of that state. Such intervention may be in pursuit of national interests unilaterally, or collectively by a group of states. Chapter I, Article 2 (7) of the UN Charter establishes the concept of "domestic jurisdiction" of the state, confirming the sanctity of the state and its right to be free from interference in its internal affairs. It states that "Nothing contained in the present Charter shall authorize the United Nations to intervene in matters which are essentially within the domestic jurisdiction of any state or shall require the Members to submit such matters to settlement under the present Charter."

Thus any intervention by the United Nations in the internal affairs of another state is not permissible, primarily because the principle of sovereignty bestows on the state complete jurisdiction in domestic affairs. However, the principle also applies to individual member states, since they have agreed to abide by the charter and its principles. In fact Article 2 (4) stipulates that "[a]ll Members shall refrain in their international relations from the threat or use of force against the territorial integrity or political independence of any state, or in any other manner inconsistent with the Purposes of the United Nations." Among the key principles stated in Article 1, the charter established the role of the Security Council in dealing with matters of international peace and security and "respect for the principle of equal rights and self-determination of peoples." It is often ignored that the principle of self-determination confers on the state the right to decide its own policy, especially where the will of the people is reflected in democratic institutions.

Compromise Approach Developed

Be that as it may, there are instances in which intervention has taken place in support of international peace and security with or without a UN mandate. It can be argued that a traditional role for peacekeeping has grown over a period of time as a compromise approach. The UN Charter only authorizes use of force under Chapter VII, should international peace and security be endangered. But intervention has also taken place under UN authority in circumstances that do not really fall within the framework of Chapter VII, and UN peacekeeping operations—often referred to as chapter six-and-a-half action—in many cases fall within this category.

The UN secretary-general once remarked very appropriately that "[p]eace-keeping can rightly be called the invention of the United Nations" (Boutros-Ghali 1995, 57). It is an invention because there is no real legal, constitutional, or structural basis for such operations, and the UN Charter has no provisions for it. This is particularly so in respect of peace enforcement within states. In many respects, peacekeeping missions have increased rapidly, partly because the Security Council has provided legitimacy to intervention in other states, as is illustrated by the comparison between what happened in Grenada (1983) and Panama (1989) with the more recent (1994) events in Haiti (Parson 1995, 267).

The expansion of peacekeeping operations in recent years, often

in direct contradiction of the UN Charter, has been creating a fundamental problem of legitimacy, particularly in the case of UN intervention in intrastate conflicts. As John Gerard Ruggie (1993, 1) says, "This
growing misuse of peacekeeping does more than strain the United Nations materially and institutionally. It has brought the world body to
the point of outright strategic failure—indeed, in Bosnia the line has
been crossed already." If the UN peacekeeping operations are to play
a meaningful role in the future, the international community shall
have to harmonize the principle of sovereignty with the need for intervention.

Disappointing UN Record

The birth of the United Nations was followed immediately by the
start of the cold war, which stymied the United Nations' ability to deal
with interstate conflicts. At the same time, its record for managing
intrastate conflicts has been mostly disappointing, mainly because of
structural limitations, the principles of sovereignty and nonintervention in domestic affairs, and the fact that the five permanent members
of the UN Security Council, especially the two superpowers, intervened
directly or indirectly in many of the conflicts. Between 1945 and 1982,
two-thirds of the conflicts were intrastate, with external intervention
a significant factor in over two-thirds of the hostilities (Kende 1978).
Superpower involvement and intervention prolonged and vitiated
many of these civil wars and intrastate conflicts, including the long
wars in Vietnam, Afghanistan, and the Horn of Africa, and only in some
cases did the United Nations try to help the state overcome the violence, as in the Congo in 1960–1961.

The United Nations, as a state-centered organization, was not designed to address the problem of internal violence and wars, and the
provisions of the UN Charter inhibit the United Nations from playing
an active role in civil wars and intrastate conflicts. Thus, even when
civil wars have expanded and involved the interests of other powers, the
United Nations has generally played a passive role. However, the frequency of UN intervention in the name of peacekeeping has increased
markedly since the end of the cold war as a result of its inability to deal
with interstate conflicts, which is its primary role.

Civil wars and the internal breakdown of states represent grave human tragedies. But their implications for international peace and security are not always clear unless there is an external involvement, and it is specifically in such cases that the United Nations has tended to shy away from involvement. During the 1990s, there were civil wars and militant violence, including sustained terrorism, in Afghanistan, Bosnia, Russia (Chechnya), Northern Ireland, India (Jammu and Kashmir), Pakistan (Sindh/Karachi), Sri Lanka, Yemen, Tajikistan, Angola, Rwanda, Somalia, and other parts of Africa, as well as in a host of other places.

In almost all these cases, outside intervention was a major factor in the escalation of violence, although not to a degree as would endanger international peace and security. After its initial enthusiasm for intervening in civil wars and contributing to humanitarian peacekeeping, the United States recognized this underlying reality, as symbolized by President Bill Clinton's address to the UN General Assembly on September 27, 1993 (Clinton 1993): "In recent weeks in the Security Council, our nation has begun asking harder questions about proposals for new peacekeeping missions: Is there a real threat to international peace? . . . The United Nations simply cannot become engaged in every one of the world's conflicts. If the American people are to say yes to UN peacekeeping, the United Nations must know when to say no." It would therefore behoove the United Nations to pay greater attention to prevention, by consciously discouraging ethnonationalism and being less permissive in providing legitimacy to separatism and secessionism, rather than after-the-fact action.

The modification of the UN's earlier peacekeeping role into what has come to be called a peace-enforcement role is a vexed question. The United Nations has often not initiated any action—except in the case of the land mines issue—in relation to the means with which the civil wars, armed militant uprisings, insurgencies, and other forms of armed violence including terrorism are fought: small arms and light weapons (Dikshit 1992–93, 205–231).

The land mines issue finally emerged on the international consciousness as a result of the attention focused by nongovernmental organizations, especially those concerned with human rights (Human Rights Watch 1993). With the possible exception of Rwanda, sophisticated weapons, such as those used by the military, have been used to spread terror and perpetrate human rights violations (Kartha 1999).

Few governments, especially in the West, are innocent of a part in the proliferation across the globe of small, highly lethal weapons which today threatens international peace and security, seriously challenges the stability of many states, and is spreading like cancer into civil society. And it should be noted that it is democratic states that are particularly vulnerable to the consequences of small arms proliferation in their societies.

Many states and substate groups have sought to use armed violence to alter the sociopolitical content of the state system in accordance with the objectives of their ideology, often based on ethnonationalism, religious radicalism, or national goals. This inevitably leads to violations of the human rights of the community, and had assumed acute proportions by the early 1990s. A great deal of small arms had been left behind by the superpowers at the end of the four-decade-long cold war, although Secretary-General Boutros Boutros-Ghali's *An Agenda for Peace* (1992) only mentions this issue in a passing reference in the follow-up report of January 1995. It is difficult to imagine how conflict situations might be managed and international peace and security bolstered today unless a concerted effort is made to curb the proliferation and use of small arms. Moreover, it is not enough that the United Nations has recognized the destabilizing influence of ethnonationalism; it must also come to grips with the problem of the political exploitation of religion and terrorism.

Moral Perceptions

Detached from the concept of sovereignty, there will always be strong moral reasons to support humanitarian intervention, particularly when gross and sustained violations of human rights or genocide occur under an extremely repressive regime or are carried out by ruling elites. Although rare, such extreme cases represent a serious dilemma, since intervention by the United Nations would still be legally and politically unjustified under the existing UN Charter which, together with the United Nations itself, is no longer in tune with geopolitical reality. As we saw in Kosovo, and to some extent in Bosnia earlier, a regional military alliance took upon itself the right to intervene when the United Nations did not possess such a right and was not likely to sanction intervention. Such actions undermined the United Nations.

INTERVENTION AND
DEVELOPING COUNTRIES

Intervention has mostly occurred in weak, developing countries, directly or through proxies, and many weak states have sought alliances and friendship with the power to ward off intervention. The reactions of developing countries in general, and India in particular, to military intervention in other countries and regions have been influenced by four factors: The specific circumstances and rationale leading to intervention; the perceived legitimacy of such an action in the eyes of the international community; the historical background that continues to shape relations between erstwhile colonial powers and the colonies that constitute the bulk of the developing countries; and the responses of countries in the region.

The incidence and frequency of military intervention by developed, industrialized states in developing countries was much greater during the cold war period than it has been since. During the cold war, many developing countries welcomed Western military intervention for such reasons as that it would prop up the regime or lend it legitimacy, be in its national security interests, or act as a counterweight against another power in the area. Nevertheless, the general attitude of developing countries was negative to intervention. Often, the Soviet Union was able to exploit this negative reaction for its own geostrategic purposes, while it intervened extensively in pursuit of its ideological goals. The overall result has been a deep-rooted suspicion in the developing world of the motives and goals of developed countries.

The Colonial Era

The historical experiences and geopolitical realities of Third World countries following three centuries of colonization have conditioned their responses to intervention. The establishment and spread of colonial empires in the South came about as a result of the major powers' military intervention, often justified in terms of "civilizing" the Asian, African, and Latin American people. Centuries of alien rule bred suspicion and mistrust of the rulers and, for many, contained bitter memories; their struggle for independence was an attempt to undo the effects of the military intervention that had created the colonial system.

The Western countries of today are mostly the imperial colonial powers of yesteryear or their allies. Even a few decades after decolonization became a widespread phenomenon, the mistrust generated during the earlier colonial era and aggravated in many cases by violent struggles for independence continues to shape the attitudes and responses of developing countries. The erosion of this trust has been increased by Western military intervention in the developing world in the postcolonial period, especially when it clearly did not have adequate legitimacy and credibility.

Cold War and Intervention

The perceived strategic objectives of rival military blocs during the cold war were a major factor in fuelling military intervention in developing countries. The extension of the logic of containment to include military intervention in internal political struggles has had a complex set of effects, the most important and lasting of which has been a sustained, deep distrust of Western intentions. The nonaligned group of countries was almost synonymous with the developing countries, which made nonalignment a response to competitive intervention. Therefore, it was inevitable that, since most of the intervention was undertaken by Western countries, the schism between the West and developing countries should grow further and continues to shape perceptions and attitudes.

Post–Cold War Intervention

One of the most important factors shaping the attitudes of developing countries will continue to be that of the legitimacy of Western intervention, much of which is undertaken under unilateral or multilateral national authority, and/or managed by the United Nations. Notwithstanding the fact that Western powers dominate the UN Security

Council (with four out of five permanent, veto-wielding powers), military intervention under the UN flag continues to be considered more legitimate than that which lacks UN authority.

The greatest opposition to Western military intervention has emerged in cases of unilateral intervention in developing countries which, under international law, is a crime specifically forbidden under Chapter I, Article 2 (4) of the UN Charter. In politico-military terms, the experience of Vietnam had also convinced the United States that unilateral intervention carries less payoffs and greater costs, which lesson the former Soviet Union learnt in Afghanistan. These experiences influenced the shift toward multilateral approaches and the use of cooperative forces, despite the fact that Chapter VII of the UN Charter defines the framework for international intervention and that any military intervention outside this framework lacks legitimacy.

Were intervention conducted at the request of a state seeking to defend itself, legitimacy would not be in question, since the UN Charter authorizes this. Thus, the U.S.-led coalition's intervention to liberate Kuwait was seen as legitimate, even though many people in developing countries felt that efforts to find a peaceful settlement had not been exhausted before the United States coalition took military action. Others believed that a UN force would have offered a better alternative and reduced the suspicion surrounding the true nature of Western intentions.

A reaction such as that of Kuwait at the time may be a rare occurrence in the future, for here was a developing country seeking Western intervention to sustain its regime; Iraqi leader Saddam Hussein was invading a sovereign state that had been a UN member for decades. From the viewpoint of the Muslim states, a powerful neighbor had suppressed the sovereignty of one of their number, yet they had not had the power to oppose the violator separately, the political and diplomatic skills to do so collectively, or the military capability to cope with Iraqi aggression. It is also possible that many states in the region preferred that the United States take the lead, so that they could avoid the responsibility of having to act militarily against a brother Muslim state.

But even though most countries of the region were deeply concerned about Saddam Hussein's violation of Kuwaiti sovereignty and the international norms that it shattered, the possibility of a similar

situation arising again is remote. Since a great deal of anguish and resistance persisted in the developing countries, especially the Muslim
states—including those that provided troops for the intervening coalition—the example of Western intervention in and on behalf of Kuwait
should not be treated as a representative model. Meanwhile, the con-
tinuing presence of Western military forces in the region, desired by
some states including Saudi Arabia, is undoubtedly feeding suspicion
and hostility such as has resulted in the terrorist attacks and violent
protests in Saudi Arabia and Bahrain.

By contrast, developing countries' support for military intervention
by the West, when conducted under UN auspices, has been more
spontaneous and widespread. Problems remain, however, when intervention has been pushed by Western powers and the United Nations
has been marginalized in the process, as happened in Kosovo.

EMERGING RESPONSES TO INTERVENTION

In the post–cold war world, various factors have aggravated the traditional mistrust of the West. The perception in Western democracies that
there is an Islamic threat has inevitably irritated not only countries
with Muslim populations, but also the developing world at large. During the past decade, the perception that there is a clash of civilizations
has inevitably drawn a line in the sand between Western countries and
those of the developing world, with future conflicts seen respectively
as wars of conscience and of interests (*Economist* 5 September 1992).
Many members of the strategic community of Western countries have
warned of threats from the South, and the world's chief superpower,
the United States, has been arguing that uncertainty has replaced the
East bloc threat of the cold war days. This is linked to defined and undefined threats from rogue states and so-called states of concern, all
essentially members of the developing world, and now the three states
anointed as comprising what U.S. President George W. Bush called the
"axis of evil." These factors have been adding to the polarization of perceptions that have increased developing countries' mistrust of Western
powers.

Since the end of the cold war, the apprehension of developing countries regarding the intentions of the West has increased, as has their

consequent sense of vulnerability because, unlike during the cold war, there is now no credible countervailing power, in spite of attempts by China to project itself in that role. Just as Western countries have increasingly come to see the behavior of developing countries as irresponsible and so requiring control, developing countries' confidence in an objective and equitable relationship with developed countries has also been eroded. The increasing role played by the Organization of the Islamic Conference (OIC) in the post–cold war era is a clear example.

The circumstances that led to intervention in the Persian Gulf in 1990–1991 are unlikely to be repeated and both direct and indirect resistance and objections can in future be expected from developing countries. It should be remembered that, even at the time of Operation Desert Storm, influential leaders like Pakistan's army chief, General Aslam Beg, were propagating the concept of strategic defiance, as symbolized by the stance taken by Saddam Hussein. While the West could well dismiss this reaction as rhetoric and posturing, and ignored it in the belief that developing countries are too weak to respond in any concrete way, the polarization of the North and South will increase and have long-term implications for international cooperation.

Developing countries are expected to seek countervailing influences to reduce the perceived negative impact of interventionary policies on their national interests. Some may adopt strategies of confrontation and opposition to Western intervention, for which postures religious ideologies and nationalist fervor could be a strong bonding factor. Those states that fail to possess the physical capability to resist intervention may resort to the use of terrorism. It may be recalled that the military leadership of the moderate Islamic country of Pakistan has long cited the Koran as legitimizing terror as a weapon to achieve victory against an enemy (Malik 1979).

The phenomenal spread of small arms and light weapons in the world has placed at the disposal of states, as well as substate and nonstate groups, the ability to impose high costs on any interventionary ground forces. While domestic popular support has become an important prerequisite for intervention by democracies, this can erode in inverse proportion to the cost of intervention in terms of lives lost, as happened with respect to Washington's intervention in Somalia. This is why Saddam Hussein fired Scud missiles into population centers in

Israel and Saudi Arabia, and why acts of terrorism might be seen as an option by countries and groups in response to Western military intervention in developing countries.

In the final analysis, it is possible to be optimistic and conclude that military intervention, except in the pursuit of national strategic interests, is likely to become less frequent in future. UN peacekeeping operations have not only reached a plateau, but are declining in frequency and levels of commitment. And even intervention in the name of such interests is likely to be restricted to ensuring access to energy resources in the Central Asia and Persian Gulf regions.

HUMANITARIAN INTERVENTION

Intervention on humanitarian grounds poses an especially difficult dilemma. The use of force for humanitarian reasons in another country, without the concurrence of its government, will inevitably result in death and destruction, and thereby carries a price tag in terms of human life. Moreover, it is uncertain how far such intervention might be successful in ameliorating the human suffering for which reason the intervention is undertaken, since the situation normally has deep-rooted causes and requires sustained effort over an extended period. Historically, the "just" war concept has provided legitimacy for the use of force, and a similar rationale could provide legitimacy for humanitarian intervention.

Broadly speaking, intervention may be seen as morally justifiable (though politically difficult) in circumstances where gross and/or sustained violations of human rights under a repressive regime takes place or genocide is perpetuated by ruling elites. Intervention on humanitarian grounds for reasons less than these take place more for strategic and political reasons than humanitarian concerns. Yet, the international community has often ignored gross violations of human rights and even genocide, having made inadequate politico-diplomatic efforts to reverse the processes. The genocide carried out by Pakistan's military forces in East Pakistan in 1971 stands out as a grim reminder of the cynicism with which the international community stood aside as over 10 million refugees fled across international borders from the terror. Rwanda is a more recent example, where hundreds of thousands of people were massacred while the international community made no effort to intervene. More to the point, there are reports that conscious efforts were made by some to ensure that the United Nations did not intervene.

It is not possible to adopt an objective approach to the issue of intervention on humanitarian grounds without examining the circumstances that lead to human rights violations at gross and sustained levels, and deciding how such violations are to be defined, with each case being judged on its individual merits. The problem is further compounded by the fact that the UN Security Council is no longer representative of the geopolitical realities of the twenty-first century and, hence, is by many not considered representative of the international community. In addition, the lack of a universally accepted definition of terrorism highlights the difficulties involved in defining human rights violations which relate to an area in which history, culture, societal values and norms, plus a host of other factors, condition people's attitudes and understanding of human rights. But, regardless of these complexities, since a general understanding can be reached that gross and sustained human rights violations are occurring, especially if genocide is involved, intervention with force to deal with such situations represents treatment of the malaise.

In the postwar era, with the single exception of the secession of East Pakistan in 1971, no group or territory claiming the right of self-determination beyond the anticolonial context achieved international recognition as a sovereign state until the fresh wave of new state formations occurred following the collapse of the Soviet Union. The case of East Pakistan is symbolic because its secession was preceded by the military ruler's refusal to honor the results of Pakistan's first constitution-based democratic election and the subsequent gross violations of human rights and genocide. India intervened unilaterally in East Pakistan, stirred into action by the influx of over 10 million refugees and the genocide that was occurring across the border in an area where a large proportion of the Indian population had family, religious, and ethnic relationships, as well as by the apathy of the international community. Even then the initial plan was to help the East Pakistani groups to take control of some territory and place them in a position to negotiate with the government in West Pakistan to find a mutually acceptable solution. But this was not to be because of the fragility of the political institutions in West Pakistan, and the unwillingness of the political, civil, and military elites to adopt democratic norms and processes, and deep ethnic prejudices. The ensuing war was one of the few "just" wars of the twentieth century and India's intervention was on humanitarian grounds.

The circumstances leading to a situation which could require intervention by the international community on humanitarian grounds may be broadly defined as follows.

Failure to Establish a State Based on the Equality of Human Beings

Almost all known cases of gross and sustained violations of human rights and genocide in the postwar period have taken place in countries where the norms supporting a social contract between the ruled and the ruler were lacking and the political system was not democratic, such as in the former Yugoslavia, Latin and Central America, Cambodia, Afghanistan, Pakistan, and Iraq.

Erosion and Failure of the State

Failure of the institutions of state invariably leads to a regression to primitive violence, especially where the culture of tolerance and mutual adjustment is weak. The examples of Afghanistan, Cambodia, Rwanda, Somalia, and the former Yugoslavia stand out.

Growing Disparities and Inequities within Society

When disparities within and among states of the North and the South become too great, particularly in the wake of rising expectations and the information revolution, the disparities give rise to a deepening sense of relative deprivation and alienation, leading to parochial groupings and even violence, as states lacking a broad-based decision-making apparatus and with a weak or absent democratic culture tend to respond with repressive policies. This often leads to gross human rights violations by the state or narrower groups, of which terrorism is an example.

Rise of Radical Ideologies, Political Exploitation of Religion

Ideological conflicts, especially those drawing their rationale and sustenance from religion and ethnicity, have been the direct cause of many major demographic shifts since 1970.

The former Yugoslavia's ethnic cleansing is a tragic example of intense post–cold war conflict. It showed all too clearly how large-scale, transnational demographic shifts can generate serious social and economic instability especially in countries suffering from economic underdevelopment and ethnic social cleavages. Then there is the nearly three-decade war in Afghanistan, that was fuelled and sustained by domestic, regional, and global ideological factors. The climax came with the Taliban regime imposing its repressive policies within, and promoting terrorism abroad in pursuit of its ideological zealotry.

Religious ideology is playing an increasing role in politics even in states that have pursued liberal democratic or socialist ideologies. International security is being affected seriously, because ". . . the combination of religion and politics is potentially explosive. The combination of religion and nationalism is stronger, but a blend of the three has an extremely destructive potential" (Falih 1991, 217).

Failure to Resolve Disputes Peacefully

This once again leads to the conclusion that democratic norms and principles would appear to hold the key to the successful management of disputes within the state and society by means of peaceful processes.

Targeting of Civil Society

Society has always been involved in war preparedness, contributing the means and manpower for wars. However, the attitudes toward civilian populations changed notably after the massive casualties of the Thirty Years War (1618–1648), and from then until the closing years of the eighteenth century, wars were less destructive to society, and were the exclusive undertaking of armies and navies. Developments arising out of the Industrial Revolution (leading to the industrialization of war) and the French Revolution (with its revolutionary nationalism), however, resulted in society itself becoming involved in war and fighting.

This coincided with the beginning of the totalitarian nature of war, which finally culminated in the world wars of the twentieth century.

World War I saw the total war model come into its own with the emergence of the political economy of war on one side, and the expansion of military-technological means to bring society totally within the fold of war on the other.

Two developments were to intensify the inclusivity of population to war. The first was the success of the Bolshevik Revolution (1917) in Russia, which established the foundations of a new revolutionary model of which the ideology of exporting revolution became an integral component. This ideology still exists, and has been pursued by other states and political entities.

The second development concerned the extension of warfare into the third dimension through the advent of air power. Rather than having to destroy an adversary's military or conquer his territory first, air warfare made it possible to target the enemy nation. The strategists of western Europe and the United States saw air power as allowing the horrors and costs of trench warfare to be avoided by penetrating an enemy's vital areas, causing such destruction and paralysis that "resistance is no longer possible and capitulation is the outcome" (Craven and Cate 1948).

During the twentieth century, the result of society having been made a prime target in warfare was that the ratio of civil-to-military casualties reversed between World War I and the Vietnam War (Swiss Federal Office of Civil Defence 1983). It may be argued that civilian casualties have been much lower in some of the more recent wars, but in the case of the Gulf War, this was not so. Iraq fired 86 Scud missiles, almost solely against population centers in Israel and Saudi Arabia, which should be seen in the context of earlier threats by Iraq to use chemical weapons. In the "war of the cities" during the Iran-Iraq War (1980–1988), over 600 ballistic missiles were fired against city centers on both sides. Missile attacks on Kabul were a perennial phenomenon for nearly a decade during the war in Afghanistan. And over 5,000 surface-to-surface missiles were fired in wars during the last five decades and, barring a few dozen, all of them targeted population centers and were perceived to have succeeded in their objective.

One of the most serious problems involving peace and security is the expansion of violence inside society for political purposes, since it not only undermines national and international security, but also threatens the human rights of civil society. This violence can be purely domestic and within national boundaries, or it may have external linkages varying from sympathy to the provision of sanctuaries or moral, political, and material support. The most commonly recognizable form is militancy and terrorism. Modern means of communication, the increased vulnerabilities of interdependent, integrated democratic civil societies, and modern instruments of violence (of which the AK-47 Kalashnikov and sophisticated explosives are symbolic) provide a powerful combination for the spread of violence.

THE LEGACY OF INTERNAL CONFLICTS

Internal wars have also often produced conditions that lead to gross human rights violations. According to Ernst B. Haas (1987), there were 102 major civil wars and colonial revolts between 1875 and 1984, out of which 77, or more than 75 percent, took place in the four decades following 1945. This indicates a marked increase in ideology-based wars, especially since fundamental alterations were wrought to the long-established Eurocentric balance of power. Kalevi J. Holsti (1991), who has examined the place of ideology in war at some length, concludes that national liberation, national unification and consolidation, and secession and state creation have caused 52 percent of the 58 wars that have occurred between 1945 and 1989. Territorial (including boundary) and ideological (including liberation) factors are noted as issues that generated war in 97 percent of the cases. In a more specific examination of the trends between 1648 and 1989, Holsti comes to the conclusion that ideology as an issue in wars has dramatically increased, especially in the more than five decades since World War II.

Barring perhaps the Gulf War, all wars and armed conflicts during the 1990s appear to have been driven substantively by ideological factors. The available empirical evidence would suggest that ideological issues and attitudes should be given greater attention if a better international security environment is to be created with less potential for human rights violations. To this end, three factors deserve special attention.

Ethnoreligious Nationalism

The world has been witnessing a growing resurgence of religion and ethnic awareness. Both factors play a useful and important role in state building, especially as an emotional anchor in an increasingly materialistic world. However, when linked to political aims and processes, strong tendencies toward nationalism defined in ethnoreligious terms are created, often ignoring civilizational and cultural identities. The break up of India, Pakistan, Yugoslavia, and the Soviet Union are in no small measure a result of this trend. Democratic polities are in a better position to manage the problems, and democracy is one of the solutions. UN Secretary General Boutros-Ghali warned that "The United Nations has not closed its door. Yet if every ethnic, religious or linguistic group claimed statehood, there would be no limit to fragmentation, and peace, security and economic well-being for all would become ever more difficult to achieve" (Boutros-Ghali 1992).

Ethnoreligious Separatist Pressures

The transnationalization of ideologies exacerbates the pressures on international stability and security, especially when attempts are made to impose ideologies by violent means. The communist ideology of exporting revolution was highly destabilizing, as is the interpretation of the concept of Muslim *um'mah* and international jihad in political terms, whereby transnational intervention and extraterritorial loyalties are sought and provide a powerful external dimension to internal disputes, with far-reaching consequences for the modern nation-state system.

As Evan Luard (1998) points out, "Often the seriousness of such (modern, localized, _civil_) wars is hugely intensified by intervention of that (external) kind. In a few cases external interference is mainly responsible for there being any war at all; as when a rebel force that would have had no significance but for outside assistance is built up to contest an existing government's rule (the Pak-created revolt in Kashmir in 1965, the US-orchestrated and financed rebellion in Nicaragua from 1981 onwards, or the South African–controlled rebellion in Mozambique today)."

The Use of Religion in Politics

The building of a state on religious foundation does not lead to stability. A case in point is what is normally referred to as Islamic fundamentalism, which is the ideology of what may perhaps be better described as the effort to establish theocentric Islamic states based on dogmatic, religious orthodoxy. Examples of such states are Iran and Pakistan which increasingly moved toward this ideological framework in the 1970s and 1980s.

"9-11" AND THE AFTERMATH

The events of September 11, 2001, have proved that Afghanistan and Pakistan have become the epicenter of international terrorism. In this connection, some points bear stressing.

1. The state as an institution in Afghanistan had been declining for three decades, with levels of violence increasing as toleration plummeted. Opportunities to reverse the process were lost.

2. Each successive regime in Kabul during the past decade indulged in increasing levels of gross violations of human rights with the international community taking little action until the terrorist acts against the United States started in 1998.

3. Religion was increasingly exploited for political purposes and narrow goals of personal ambition, as well as to legitimize violence and repression.

4. Terror and violence were increasingly employed as instruments of politics.

5. Cross-border terrorism sponsored and supported by states, including the Taliban and its mentor, Pakistan, emerged as a new form of intervention. It was designed to achieve political goals and was presented in the guise of religious ideology.

6. The use of force by U.S.-led coalition forces to dismantle the repressive, terrorist regime of the Taliban represented intervention that can be categorized as a "just" war and humanitarian intervention, in which care was taken to ensure that the use of force and collateral damage would be kept to a minimum in a sophisticated multi-dimensional, politico-diplomatic-military campaign.

CONCLUSION

The foregoing study looks at intervention, which it defines as the use of force by a state or organization inside another state without the latter's concurrence. At the same time, it shows how, while it may not be possible to arrive at a rigid definition of gross violations of human rights, genocide is more easily defined.

In principle preventive steps provide greater payoff than post-violation use of force. Situations requiring external intervention to stop genocide or gross violations of human rights from being carried out by a regime normally can be forecast in advance, allowing adequate scope for timely corrective action. Most of the circumstances necessitating possible external intervention arise in countries where the nation-state has either greatly weakened, is eroding to the level of near failure, or is being governed by brute force without a mass-support base. Long-term preventive measures against violations of human rights need to be based on the promotion of the democratic principle and the rule of law and justice, sustaining and strengthening of the nation-state system and the peaceful resolution of disputes.

Intervention may be seen to be morally justifiable in the rare event that gross or sustained violations of human rights are carried out under an extremely repressive regime, or genocide is perpetuated by ruling elites. But intervention is politically and legally justified only on humanitarian grounds if the human rights violations represent a threat to international peace and security, as defined in Chapter VII of the UN Charter, or in the case of self-defense. The challenge facing the international community is how to legitimize humanitarian intervention.

The UN Security Council represents a geopolitical system that is obsolete, yet there has been strong resistance to reforming the UN system. Meanwhile, should circumstances continue to exist in which intervention with force is necessary and even desirable, it would be necessary to ensure that the use of force is kept to a minimum. Above all, the legitimacy of any intervention will remain critical, and would necessitate the concurrence of the majority of the states in the international community. This could best be achieved by requiring that a defined minimum number of member states of the United Nations approve any UN Security Council proposal, or that of any particular state or group of states, for intervention.

The sovereign-state system, in spite of its limitations and faults, is still the only viable form of organization in the world. The central objective of the international community to deal with human rights violations should be to prevent circumstances from arising in which the state is not built or managed in accordance with the principles of the equality, liberty, and fraternity of all human beings living therein. State sovereignty often provides the opportunity for ruling elites to initiate repressive policies. Paradoxically, the circumstances which could lead to situations in which gross violations of human rights take place (and, hence, create the necessity for intervention) essentially arise from failures to build states on democratic principles. If humanitarian violations are to be systematically dealt with, it will be necessary to ensure that the state, as an institution, is strengthened.

Any intervention must be constructed on an unambiguous commitment publicly stating that the territorial integrity and viability of the target state will be upheld. This means that state borders would remain inviolable. In the event that territories are disputed among states, the international community must insist that mutually agreed lines of control should not be disturbed by direct or indirect use of force, and that they should remain inviolable until the dispute has been peacefully settled. The international community must remain vigilant lest one state intervene in the domestic affairs of another through nonstate actors in a bid to alter the nature of the state or its territory on ideological grounds or for political aims.

BIBLIOGRAPHY

Boutros-Ghali, Boutros. 1992. "An Agenda for Peace: Preventive Diplomacy, Peacemaking and Peace-keeping." Report of the Secretary-General pursuant to the statement adopted by the Summit Meeting of the Security Council on 31 January 1992. <http://www.un.org/Docs/SG/agpeace.html> (28 November 2002).

———. 1995. *An Agenda for Peace 1995*. Second edition. New York: United Nations.

Clinton, Bill. 1993. Address by the President to the 48th Session of the United Nations General Assembly (27 September).

Craven, W. F., and J. B. Cate, eds. 1948. *The Army Air Forces in World War II*. Chicago: University of Chicago Press.

Dikshit, Prashant. 1992–93. "Proliferation of Small Arms and Minor Weapons." *Asian Strategic Review*. New Delhi: Institute for Defense Studies and Analyses.

Falih Abd al Jabbar. 1991. "The Gulf War and Ideology: The Double-edged Sword of Islam." In Haim Bresheeth and Nira Yuval-Davis, eds. *The Gulf War and the New World Order*. London: Zed Books.

Haas, Ernst B. 1987. "War, Interdependence and Functionalism." In Raimo Vayrynen. *The Quest for Peace: Transcending Collective Violence and War among Societies, Cultures and States*. London: Sage Publications, Ltd.

Holsti, Kalevi J. 1991. *Peace and War: Armed Conflicts and International Order*. Cambridge, U.K.: Cambridge University Press.

Human Rights Watch. 1993. *Landmines: A Deadly Legacy*. New York: Human Rights Watch.

Jackson, Robert. 1999. "Sovereignty in World Politics: A Glance at the Conceptual and Historical Landscape." In Robert Jackson, ed. *Sovereignty at the Millennium*. Malden, Mass.: Blackwell Publishers.

Kartha, Tara. 1999. *Tools of Terror*. New Delhi: Knowledge World.

Kende Istvan. 1978. "Wars of Ten Years (1967–76)." *Journal of Peace Research* 15(3): 227–241.

———. 1983. "New Features of Armed Conflicts and Armament in Developing Countries." *Development and Peace* (Spring).

Luard, Evan. 1988. *The Blunted Sword: The Erosion of Military Power in Modern World Politics*. London: I. B. Tauris.

Malik, Brigadier S. K. 1979. *Quranic Concept of War*. Lahore: Wajidalis.

Parson, Anthony. 1995. *From Cold War to Hot Peace: UN Interventions 1947–1994*. London: Michael Joseph.

Ruggie, John Gerard. 1993. "The United Nations: Stuck in a Fog Between Peacekeeping and Enforcement." In William H. Lewis, ed. *Peacekeeping: The Way Ahead?* McNair Paper 25. Washington, D.C.: National Defense University Press.

Swiss Federal Office of Civil Defence. 1983. *Civil Defence: Figures, Facts, Data—1983/84*. Berne: Swiss Federal Office of Civil Defence.

6. ASEAN

Simon S. C. Tay and Rizal Sukma

HUMANITARIAN intervention is a significant aspect of a wider and growing challenge to the notion of state sovereignty. International convention has it that all states are sovereign and equal, and that the primary legitimate actor in international relations is the state. In the name of the state, its government or regime is the sole authority to speak and act concerning areas of bilateral, regional, and global cooperation. This convention continues into the present day. However, trends in globalization, such as the dissemination of knowledge and growing economic interdependence, are increasing the need for each state to be cognizant of other states' activities. At the same time, the relevance of, and space set aside for, nonstate actors has widened the agenda for cooperation beyond the narrower interests of the state and regime, to include broader human concerns.

As a result, new sources of tension have arisen among states as well as within regional and international regimes. While some continue to honor and give priority to the sanctity of state sovereignty as an ordering principle of the international community, others are increasingly evoking what they claim are universal tenets in the belief that there are exceptions to the principle of state sovereignty.

We might ask whether any one state or group of states has a right to interfere or intervene in another state using either coercion or force. If the answer is in the affirmative, we might further ask on what basis and under what conditions intervention could be justified, and whether human rights considerations or other alleged universal principles would justify intervention.

The controversy surrounding the intervention in Kosovo by the North Atlantic Treaty Organisation (NATO) in the spring of 1999 triggered these and other questions, and demonstrated the tension existing between state sovereignty and claims of legitimate intervention. Thus, while the nations of Southeast Asia were neither directly affected by NATO's bombing of Belgrade, ostensibly conducted to champion human rights, nor defenders of the atrocities in the former Yugoslavia that had preceded the NATO action, they have been the venue of considerable debate regarding the broader implications of humanitarian intervention on state sovereignty that reaches far beyond the particular concerns in Kosovo. The possibility that so-called solutions might be imposed on smaller, weaker Southeast Asian states by larger, more powerful states remains a major concern for three main reasons.

First, U.S. primacy in military and other affairs in the early years of the twenty-first century has merged with unilateralist impulses under the presidency of George W. Bush since the terrorist attacks in the United States on September 11, 2001 (Brooks and Wohlforth, 2002; "Present" 2002). This has increased concern that the United States, unilaterally or with a small number of allies, may chose to intervene and use force in another country on the pretext of defending either human rights or some other international norm. Such fears remain. Even while the bombing of Belgrade recedes further into the past, discussions about Western or American-led intervention in the name of protecting human rights or promoting democracy were rekindled in 2002, when the Amercian-led war on Iraq was being discussed (Tay 2002).

Second, many Southeast Asian governments still regard the principles of noninterference or nonintervention as vital for regional stability and cooperation. Not only has state sovereignty been central to the development of relations within the Association of Southeast Asian Nations (ASEAN), but it is a key principle in the so-called ASEAN way, considered a necessary factor even in relations with non-ASEAN states.[1]

Third, the principle of nonintervention is becoming an increasingly pertinent factor in the region, given both the changing nature of the regional and global security environment since the end of the cold war, and the rapid domestic globalization-related transformations in some key regional countries.

Discussion concerning state sovereignty, cooperation, and intervention initially began as a dialogue within the foreign policy community at the track-two level, but has now entered the domain of official debate. ASEAN's struggle to come to terms with the issues has been clearly demonstrated in the discussions held since late 1997 on such key concepts as constructive intervention, constructive involvement, flexible engagement, constructive engagement, and enhanced interaction.

This chapter explores a range of ASEAN views and is divided into three sections. The first looks at the changing context of nonintervention debate in ASEAN, and explores ASEAN views regarding NATO's humanitarian intervention in Kosovo (Sukma 2000; Tay 2001). The second section discusses the relationship between sovereignty and human rights in ASEAN. The third presents a sketch of ASEAN views, which are quite diverse in nature and perspectives, and considers the overarching ASEAN view on the issues of force, sovereignty, and intervention. In conclusion, some thoughts are offered on the evolution of rules and norms in international relations and what ASEAN member states might do in the future.

SOVEREIGNTY AND NONINTERVENTION

The origins of state sovereignty are most commonly traced back to the 1648 Peace of Westphalia that ended the Thirty Years' War against the Holy Roman Empire. The concept of the state is a recent accretion in the Southeast Asian political arena, a product of colonization and subsequent independence. It supplants prior, precolonial notions held by civilizations and kingdoms of indefinite territorial reach, and is useful in view of the region's various territorial issues, as well as the cross-border influences of race and religion. On independence, the ASEAN member states adopted the Westphalian system of the state, and have strengthened and reinforced it with their adoption of the norm of nonintervention and their resultant, accompanying practices. In ASEAN, for example, it is not only the use of force—or the threat that it might be used—that is construed as intervention; even public criticism may be considered interference or intervention and, thus, be rejected.

The state-centric norms of Asian and ASEAN states have led some to liken regional relations to those of nineteenth-century Europe (Kissinger 2002).[2] By contrast, European states have for some time been pooling their sovereignty in the complex experiment of the European Union. This has led some to describe Europe as moving toward a post-sovereign state. U.S. foreign policy is increasingly emphasizing inter-dependent global concerns that elude states and their sovereign borders in policy areas such as security and terrorism, trade and economic ties, human rights and democracy, as well as corruption and governance. This has implications for sovereignty in other states. ASEAN, however, has only recently started to question the adoption and adaptation of strict forms of state sovereignty, and then only at the prodding of a number of factors.

The first consideration is foreign and global in nature. As a result of the changing nature of post–cold war international relations, there developed a need to reassess the relevance of nonintervention. The end of the geopolitical rivalry between the United States and the Soviet Union allowed a greater recognition of other factors and helped accelerate the processes of globalization. In an ever more complex world, maintaining the analytical distinction and separation between domestic and international issues has become increasingly artificial and difficult. Issues such as human rights, democratization, and the environment have become prominent in interstate relations and have opened up the boundaries between domestic and international realms.

In the eyes of many Western countries, such boundaries no longer exist and, whether those in other parts of the world like it or not, these states have begun to make these issues core elements in their foreign policies (Sukma 1997). ASEAN member states, both collectively and individually, have had to find ways of dealing with these concerns. The Asian human rights debate, in which a number of ASEAN leaders have prominently participated, may be seen as one example of their response to this post–cold war agenda (Tay 1996). Yet, even given that the rethinking of sovereignty was kickstarted by considerations of foreign origin, subsequent deliberation has been spawned in the ASEAN region, by various countries and sectors of national society.

A second factor in the questioning of the strictures of state sovereignty is the growing recognition of transboundary incidents within Southeast Asia that have come to be seen as nontraditional sources of interstate insecurity and instability. These problems include the growing incidence of piracy, disputes over fishing grounds, the burgeoning illegal trade in people, drugs, weapons, and other contraband, as well as environmental disasters, and marine pollution. Efforts to address these issues challenge the strict sense of state sovereignty because what one state does within its own territory can, and frequently does, cause external, transboundary harm to its neighbors. This increases the need for states to cooperate or, when that does not occur, for other states to consider some form of suasion, sanctions, or intervention to elicit cooperation and prevent damage.

Of the transboundary problems, environmental issues have come to occupy a special place in contemporary ASEAN discourse on nonconventional security threats. A case in point are the repeated forest fires in Indonesia (Tay 1999b) that have received special attention from regional countries due to the unprecedented scale of the fires and their devastating impact beyond Indonesia's borders on neighboring countries including Brunei, Malaysia, and Singapore. In 2002, ASEAN sought to address the issue through a treaty that, while not yet in force and yet to be proved effective, is noteworthy as a rare step for the grouping, which has tended to emphasize action plans and political declarations. Moreover, in the interests of our discussion of sovereignty and intervention, it should be noted that the treaty addresses issues concerning forest and fire policies within a state, a matter that would normally be considered domestic and solely under the sovereign control of the state (Tay 2002). The intra-ASEAN debate about sovereignty has been fueled by the recognition of shared, transboundary concerns within Southeast Asia, and of other nontraditional security concerns.

The third factor that has strengthened the pressure on the principles of state sovereignty and noninterference is a growing awareness of the regional impact that can arise from instabilities and conflict in national politics. One unfortunate development that triggered this awareness concerns the 1997 outbreak of conflict in Cambodia between Hun Sen and Norodom Ranaridh. Some argued that the failure of Cambodia to sustain internal peace and the reconstruction process was caused by the inadequate role played by ASEAN in helping the country overcome its domestic problems. Then-Deputy Prime Minister of Malaysia Anwar Ibrahim, for example, argued that, "our non-involvement in the reconstruction of Cambodia actually contributes to the deterioration and final collapse of national reconciliation" (Anwar 1997). Within that context, he proposed the idea of constructive intervention that, in turn, set the pace for official debate on the issue in ASEAN government circles. It is important, however, to note that constructive intervention is meant as "a policy of proactive involvement and assistance to Southeast Asia's weaker nations with a view to preventing their internal collapse" (Rajaretnam 1999, 46). In the event, ASEAN did not admit Cambodia as a full member until it had made arrangements for a compromise that, meeting the major concerns of the rival parties, would ensure power sharing and peaceful accommodation. ASEAN was unwilling to accept state sovereignty as an excuse to ignore national-level conflict and so "interfered" in Cambodia and legitimized that interference.

Then there is the question of Myanmar. Heavy criticism of its human rights record by Western and some other governments did not deter ASEAN acceptance of Myanmar as a member in 1997. This was a clear manifestation of the noninterference principle as, in defending its decision, ASEAN maintained that the criteria for membership are not based on a country's domestic conditions. In addition, however, ASEAN also argued that Myanmar's membership of the group would open up the opportunity for ASEAN to induce some changes in that country's domestic political situation through the exercise of constructive engagement. While it is hard to imagine how ASEAN might induce changes without being seen to have interfered in Myanmar's internal affairs, its evasion of sovereignty enabled it to accept Myanmar into the fold. Events in Myanmar since then have again impacted on ASEAN practice. In mid-2003, as part of their annual meeting and statement, ASEAN foreign ministers made an exceptional expression of concern over the situation in Myanmar, where the governing regime has redetained the pro-democracy leader, Aung San Suu Kyi. Again, however, the statement was not seen to directly override ASEAN norms, as the statement was endorsed by all ASEAN member states by consensus, including Myanmar.

Other recent examples of the trend to exercise constructive engagement can be found in Indonesia, in the wake of the 1997 economic crisis. In East Timor, the human rights violations carried out by the militia after the referendum for independence triggered shock and concern across the region and the world. While ASEAN member states did not feature strongly in the initial intervention by the multinational force led by Australia in September 1999, they did participate and, later, led the United Nations (UN) peacekeeping mission in February 2002. Moreover, although the UN mission did obtain the consent of the Indonesian government under then-president B. J. Habibie prior to entering East Timor, many Indonesians resented the international and, especially, Australian actions, which they labeled intervention.[3]

In addition, the actions carried out during 1998 in Indonesia by mobs and other forces against ethnic–Chinese Indonesians triggered responses that have had implications for the ASEAN debate on sovereignty and nonintervention. The nature and scale of the human-rights violations triggered reactions in many countries around the world, including those with Chinese populations. In neighboring Singapore, for example, while the government did not interfere with, or officially complain to, its Indonesian counterpart, civil-society groups expressed concern and protested to the Indonesian embassy. In these times, when information flows readily across borders and civil-society groups are freer to act, state sovereignty no longer serves as a shield to deflect criticism and interference.

The above examples show that human-rights concerns are no longer matters pertinent only to states outside the grouping, and that they can and do trigger reactions among Southeast Asians. As a result, policies and actions may change, either as in the cases of Cambodia and Myanmar, in which the government represented the state, or as a result of the activities of civil society and other sectors of the public. Even in Southeast Asia the principle of state sovereignty no longer justifies the view that any one state is a black box, impenetrable to the gaze and concerns of other states.

The fourth factor touching on the principles of state sovereignty and noninterference is the changing nature of ASEAN as an institution. For more than three decades, ASEAN has been very much a state-centric regional institution, primarily defined by the political elite of its member states and reflecting their common reality that the state is the dominant, if not the only, author of foreign policy agendas. That reality is a logical consequence of the nature of state-society relations in many ASEAN countries, in which the state has assumed dominance over society. However, some change has become evident in the wake of the start of the Southeast Asian economic crisis in 1997.

This crisis and its attendant domestic political consequences have altered ASEAN's regional and national political context. The current move to strengthen civil society in a number of ASEAN countries such as Indonesia, Thailand, and the Philippines has altered the relationship between the state and society. The demands of civil society and other sectors of society for a greater role in politics and the policy-making process are increasingly more difficult for the state to resist. While most observations about civil society have emphasized its growing role at the domestic and national levels, its expanding role in shaping regional relations should not be ignored.

An example of this is the earlier-mentioned civil-society protests against the Indonesian government over the violation of the human rights of ethnic Chinese Indonesians in 1998. Other instances of civil-society concerns that transcend sovereign borders are being seen in different contexts, even outside the realm of human rights. In part, this is linked to the growing emergence of civil-society groups that transact across borders in Asia and ASEAN.[4]

Indeed, the rise of nonstate actors in individual states has paralleled the growing importance of transnational issues—such as democracy, human rights, and the environment—in the agenda of both nongovernmental organizations (NGOs) and states. As a result of the growing interdependence of ASEAN states, events occurring in the domestic domain of any single member state are bound to have an impact on other member states.

There are clear regional implications for the principle of nonintervention in particular, and ASEAN in general. On the one hand, civil societies have either brought pressure to bear on their respective governments to address human rights violations in other countries, or at least shown that they have clear views on such cases. They have themselves raised the issues by condemning and criticizing what they perceive to be human rights violations, regardless of where they have occurred. This indicates that the notion of national sovereignty is no longer a barrier to expressing concern about events beyond their respective national boundaries. On the other hand, however, states are obliged to refrain from intervening in another sovereign country's domestic domain.

Intervention, perceived or actual, often leads to heightening tension between and among states. Protest marches, the burning of flags, and some acts of violence against embassies have been seen in Indonesia in the post-Suharto period. Acts against citizens of another country—such as the threatened targeting of U.S. citizens in Indonesia—can be another source of interstate tension and possible diplomatic incidents.

ASEAN attitudes to, and practices regarding, state sovereignty have shifted and remain in a state of flux. While this may be welcome for many, it cannot be said that the path forward is certain, uncomplicated, and without bumps and possible pitfalls.

Yet, while state sovereignty is being debated within ASEAN, there remain a number of reservations about the activities of NATO in Kosovo. This is because, although ASEAN governments and their peoples still find areas in which they do not treat state sovereignty as absolute, they have preferred modes of increased cooperation, political suasion, and possible criticism. Their methods of dealing with the balance between sovereignty and interdependence have, however, very clearly avoided the use of coercion and military force. Thus, of the many dimensions in the disquiet about NATO action in Kosovo, the elements of coercion and force are central concerns.

Many ASEAN countries, being mainly small to medium-sized states, have reservations about the use of coercion and force, which attract their almost instinctive protest and suspicion. Often, coercion and force are viewed in the region as the exercise of power politics, rather than a legal act or moral requirement. Indeed, the early development of ASEAN was itself primarily an effort to end the use of coercion and force in intrastate relations in the region. This was initially related to efforts to end Indonesia's policy of confrontation toward Malaysia and Singapore, after Sukarno had been replaced at the helm in Jakarta in 1966, and later to various other territorial disputes between and among ASEAN member states. This ASEAN way may be understood as a construct to ensure peaceful coexistence among the ASEAN member states, even though it might be seen as having shortcomings as a basis for closer cooperation. ASEAN member states as a whole uphold present-day international law and insist there are now strict limits to the legitimate use of force.[5]

In addition, some ASEAN member states—especially Indonesia and Malaysia—have been leading members of the nonaligned movement and are generally very wary of big-power intervention. The ASEAN idea of there being a Zone of Peace, Freedom and Neutrality (ZOPFAN) may be viewed as a construct opposed to such intervention, as well as the use and presence of military force, and is still considered important by some. This is despite the fact that two ASEAN member states—the Philippines and Thailand—are formal allies of the United States, and that Manila, which previously hosted large numbers of U.S. military forces, has since 2001 engaged U.S. military advisers on its territory. As some have noted, while the states of ASEAN shelter under U.S. protection and depend for their security on its continued presence and interest in the region, many insist on a declaration of nonalignment (Kissinger 2002, 114).

From this perspective, any exercise of force on the scale that was seen in Kosovo must necessarily come under close scrutiny. Most states in ASEAN and, indeed, elsewhere disapprove of the fact that the NATO allies failed to even seek, let alone obtain, specific UN authorization before intervening. Bereft of these elements of UN consent and consultation, the NATO actions are viewed by most in ASEAN as having been unilateral and prima facie illegal under existing international law. Even had the UN Security Council been unable to act, as most expected, because of a veto by Russia or China, the process would have tested world opinion more fully.[6] Extending this counter-factual argument allows one to more clearly see the views of ASEAN member states.

If the United States and its European allies had gone to the United Nations before acting, the process would have been reassuring for most ASEAN member states which, generally speaking, tend to emphasize the importance of international law and the opinion of states as expressed in the United Nations. Indeed, a number of them have been active in the United Nations and as nonpermanent members of the UN Security Council. Specifically on the question of Kosovo, a number of ASEAN member states, including Malaysia, had plaintively expressed concern regarding the atrocities perpetrated in the states of the former Yugoslavia, especially where these had been visited on Muslims. Along with other states, they had criticized the West for years of inaction and urged that they act. Thus, had the United States and its allies sought their views before acting through NATO, a number of ASEAN member states might even have had some sympathy for the subsequent actions. Certainly, the tension between their previous calls for action would have had to be balanced by their concerns over the legitimacy of the intervention.

As it was, NATO was seen to act without consultation and unilaterally, notwithstanding its regional character. Because of this, many states in the United Nations, including some in ASEAN, enjoyed the freedom of criticizing the intervention without much regard to either what they would have done or the consequences of inaction. They were able, as they had before, to criticize the NATO action, even while they believed it just might help curb the atrocities that were being played out in the former Yugoslavia.

Another and quite different basis from which some in ASEAN viewed the NATO actions with disquiet relates to fairness and effectiveness. ASEAN member states have noted that NATO did not initially act in the former Yugoslavia against the military forces and militia that were perpetrators of crimes against ethnic minorities. Rather, their bombing of Belgrade exposed civilian populations to danger. So-called smart bombs did not always prevent harm from being caused to the innocent, as the bombing of the Chinese Embassy in Belgrade showed. Some in ASEAN also derided the Western alliance's refusal to deploy ground troops, and did not believe that the cause could be won exclusively by aerial campaigns. Given the denouement in the former Yugoslavia and the ongoing trial of former Serbian leader Slobodan Milosevic, these criticisms have quietened, although events in the region are still being watched by some who see them as an indication of Western democracies' commitment to building peace in the region following the NATO intervention.

As these incidents are geographically remote for many in ASEAN, memories of the initial opposition to NATO intervention are fading. To understand the underlying currents of thinking on related issues, rather than merely on this incident, it is necessary to consider two landmark events in the ASEAN region.

The first and more recent event is the earlier-mentioned action led by Australia in East Timor. Technically, consent was given by the Habibie government, and this was not a case of intervention. Nevertheless, there has been considerable resentment among Indonesians at many levels and in many sectors of the country, because consent was given under considerable pressure, and Australia was seen as precipitate in offering to lead the effort.

While some ASEAN states are of the view that events in East Timor could not and should not have been condoned, they did not take immediate part in the Australian action. This was primarily because they lacked ready capacity and out of respect for Indonesian sentiment. An important underlying factor is, however, that the projection of force and coercion among ASEAN member states remains unacceptable. This explains why, although they had not responded earlier, a number of ASEAN member states later played significant roles in the UN's East Timor effort.

The second event in the regional experience that has shaped attitudes about intervention and sovereignty is the Vietnamese invasion of Cambodia in 1978, when there was concern that the Pol Pot regime was responsible for the conduct of genocide in what has come to be called "the killing fields." None in ASEAN either excused such acts by the state against its own citizens, nor regretted the expulsion of the Pol Pot regime.

Nevertheless, the intervention was not welcomed by ASEAN member states. There was concern that the Vietnamese invasion would not be a limited intervention to protect human rights and stem the outward flow of refugees that was destabilizing many surrounding countries. In the context of the cold war and the Vietnam conflict, most feared that the invasion was a first step in Vietnamese expansion. The domino theory held that Vietnam, supported by the Soviet Union, would expand its territory and influence from South Vietnam and Cambodia through Thailand and down into the Malay peninsula.

Thus, ASEAN member states campaigned, strongly and largely in concert, against the intervention and to oust the regime installed by Vietnam, which had not yet become an ASEAN member state. Indeed, the campaign served as a rallying point for ASEAN members and is one of the high points of their external diplomacy.

In the intervening decades, the issue has been resolved with the normalization of ties with Vietnam and its 1995 entry into the association. The Paris Peace Accords in the post–cold war period have also paved the way for elections in Cambodia, as well as its admission to ASEAN in 1999. Yet the issue has shaped ASEAN, bolstering the attachment to the norm of nonintervention. For many of those member states that opposed Vietnam's actions, it serves as a reminder that what some may call "humanitarian intervention" can be used to mask ulterior motives for the use of force.

SOVEREIGNTY AND HUMAN RIGHTS

The claim of humanitarian intervention is not that the use of force is acceptable for any reason. Rather, it is a claim that there is another exception to the general prohibition against one state using force against another, in addition to self-defense and acts sanctioned by the United Nations. The new exception claimed by the proponents of humanitarian intervention is for the protection of human beings against gross and widespread violations of their rights, especially mass killing, genocide, and acts that can be considered crimes against humanity. The attitude of a state to the idea of humanitarian intervention can, therefore, be seen as a balance between the belief in sovereignty and the prohibition against the use of force on one hand and, on the other, the respect and importance it attaches to the protection of human rights.

In the case of Kosovo, the United States and its NATO allies have been among the vocal proponents of human rights. Many sectors of public opinion in Europe in fact saw a need for their governments to take some form of action long before the bombing of Belgrade took place. In the case of Germany, a central economic and political actor in Europe although not a major military power, the urge to support actions in Kosovo was linked both to the protection of human rights and to its own history: Many Germans believed that their country and its European partners could not remain inert in the face of ethnic cleansing that paralleled the violations of World War II against Jews and other minorities. Here it would be useful to survey ASEAN attitudes to the protection of human rights before considering the question of balancing sovereignty, force, and intervention.

As a whole but with some exceptions, ASEAN member states have not been as vocal in promoting human rights as have Western democracies. As already noted, ASEAN as a group put cold war politics before concerns about the Pol Pot regime in protesting the Vietnamese invasion of Cambodia and seeking a diplomatic solution to remove the regime installed by the Vietnamese.

In the post–cold war period, too, as already briefly noted, some ASEAN member states and their leaders have played a prominent role in the Asian values debate, which holds that Asian culture and development needs legitimize a different standard in human rights and democracy. There are grounds, at least in certain ASEAN states, to argue that some aspects of human rights demonstrate a bias toward Western heritage. This is especially true in the emphasis placed on civil and political rights as compared to that on economic, social, and cultural rights. Many international documents and prominent experts acknowledge that these different types of human rights should be equal and indivisible. However, in practice, most governments in the West and almost all Western-based NGOs focus on civil and political human rights to the exclusion of the other rights (Tay 1996).

ASEAN member states have not played major roles in the expansion of human rights treaties at the international level, although some of the states have been active on UN human rights commissions. Nor are all of them close followers. For example, the only human rights treaties to enjoy widespread acceptance among ASEAN member states are those relating to the Convention on the Rights of the Child, and the Convention on the Elimination of All Forms of Discrimination against Women (CEDAW). In contrast, the International Covenant on Civil and Political Rights (ICCPR) has been accepted only by a small minority of ASEAN member states.

Within ASEAN itself, the picture is mixed. There has been an increase in the number of institutions for human rights in some ASEAN member states. National human rights commissions now exist in the Philippines, Indonesia, Malaysia, and Thailand, while three human rights institutions are linked to different organs of state in Cambodia. There remains, however, no regional human rights mechanism for ASEAN.[7] This is in contrast to the regional mechanisms in Europe, the Americas, and Africa. ASEAN has mentioned human rights commitments in some of its documents and declarations, including the wide-ranging Hanoi Plan of Action to implement the ASEAN Vision 2020. However, there is no regular and official ASEAN coordination or forum for human rights, which is in sharp contrast to the many other areas in which there is cooperation, such as economic concerns.

In general, ASEAN member states uphold the norm of nonintervention and are reluctant to do or say anything that might be construed as interference in the domestic affairs of another state. Nevertheless, it is notable that more in ASEAN have increasingly come to accept that the principle of state sovereignty, enshrined in Article 2 (7) of the Charter of the United Nations, cannot be allowed to shield gross and widespread abuses of human rights carried out by a state against its own people. There are arguments of law and precedent that lead ASEAN to concede this. After all, the promotion of human rights (UN Charter, Arts. 55 and 56) is a stated purpose of the United Nations, just as are peace and development (UN Charter, Art. 1 [3]). Moreover, the origins of the United Nations in the post–World War II period and its actions in condemning South Africa's apartheid demonstrate that human rights are now a legitimate concern for the international community.

However, many in ASEAN would hold that the process, institutions, and instruments for demonstrating and acting on that international concern are critical. Where the United Nations authorizes or instructs, compulsory sanctions (as in the case of South Africa) or even the use of force can be legitimated. There are also other UN procedures and treaty bodies that monitor, review, and report on human rights abuses by states, exposing them to criticism. In these circumstances, the multilateral character of the institutions and processes give greater legitimacy to the process of some states expressing concern about human rights in a particular state or, indeed, taking collective action against that state.

In contrast, there are many concerns about the unilateral imposition of sanctions and pressure in the name of human rights. ASEAN states have been quite uniform in speaking out against such unilateral impositions by Western democracies or international institutions that attach human rights as conditions for the granting of aid and the conduct of trade. Most in ASEAN would criticize such sanctions on the basis of their subjectivity and unfairness. The sanctions are decided by one state, often reacting to its own domestic constituencies, and are often subjective and inconsistent. Unilateral action is also possible in the case of powerful states, while smaller and medium-sized states do not have this option.

As such, while ASEAN is not a vocal champion of human rights, it avoids both an absolutist approach to sovereignty, and allowing any and all unilateral actions that evoke the name of human rights. Rather, decisions are taken on a case-by-case basis, since institutions and processes matter for ASEAN.

Another factor that has increased the weight that ASEAN member states give human rights protection is the rejection of authoritarian regimes and the growth of democracy in the region. The Philippines has, since the ouster of President Ferdinand Marcos, been a vocal advocate of democracy and human rights, even when others in the region sought to legitimize Asian values and differences. In Cambodia, too, since the UN administration of the country, human rights has been seen to be part of the country's path forward. Thailand has increasingly come to identify the legitimacy of its government with elections, democracy, and the protection of human rights, as set out in its latest constitution. Under the previous government, led by Prime Minister Chuan Leekpai and as represented by Minister of Foreign Affairs Surin Pitsuwan, Thai foreign policy was also beginning to express and externalize concerns about human rights and democracy, especially in the case of neighboring Myanmar.

Yet while these three countries are not inconsiderable influences in ASEAN, perhaps the most significant change has come in Indonesia, since the end of the Suharto regime. In Indonesia today, especially among the nongovernmental sectors, human rights and democracy are emphasized, with the focus on internal concerns at the local and national level. Some of this attention, however, has turned outward to concerns in the region. While Indonesian foreign policy does not at present manifest these concerns about human rights, trends in this direction should be anticipated if the country does, indeed, become entrenched in a more democratic ethos with an emphasis on human rights.

Elsewhere in ASEAN, changes pointing to a greater and more articulated promotion of democracy and human rights have been more limited. Yet other ideals and ideas do tend in the same direction. One example is in the field of security. Here, the legitimacy of looking at the treatment of people within states is magnified if one considers that it is not only state security that matters, but also the security of the individual human being. This idea of human security, increasingly propounded by some countries in Asia Pacific, is allied to human rights and forces one to look more critically at the risks faced by the individual.

Another example is in the field of good governance, which has been upheld as a prerequisite for the recovery of ASEAN economies and their progress toward fuller human and economic development. Embedded in the idea of good governance, along with non-corrupt practices and other issues, is the protection of at least basic human rights.

The majority of ASEAN member states are still not vocal champions of human rights and, even among those that do believe in such rights, there is a reluctance to voice strong public criticism of neighbors and a still stronger aversion to the use of coercion and force. Thus, while the matter of human rights has come more clearly onto the ASEAN agenda in recent years, it does not strongly militate toward the acceptance of humanitarian intervention.

HUMANITARIAN INTERVENTION

To speak of an ASEAN view on humanitarian intervention or almost any other topic is often difficult because ASEAN is neither a single state nor a union of states as is, for example, the European Union. It is, rather, an association that often has no common position on issues. This aspect remains the essence of ASEAN, notwithstanding a growing recognition of the need for greater cooperation, particularly in the economic sphere, and even calls to reinvent ASEAN (Tay et al. 2001).

Thus far, this chapter has looked at some of the mainstream views that some or a majority of ASEAN member states may hold on issues. To some degree, differences between ASEAN member states, as well as between government and nongovernment sectors, have also been noted. In this section, the diversity in ASEAN is considered in order to present an idea of the range of ASEAN opinions on sovereignty and intervention.

To this end, three interlinking factors should be considered. First, the extent to which a society believes in democracy and human rights, and the degree to which civil-society groups influence state policy. Second, the extent to which the state is and feels itself to be interdependent with its neighbors. Third, the ability of the state to protect itself against intervention by another state, including its neighbors as well as the United States and its allies.

In looking at democracy, human rights, and civil society, we must recognize that ASEAN member states are becoming increasingly differentiated. The Asian crisis that swept the region brought varying degrees of democracy to ASEAN states, and in some cases democracy has not proved effective or acceptable. Thus we see that the governments or leaders in the Philippines and Thailand changed in early 2001, and that President Abdurrahman Wahid of Indonesia was replaced by President Megawati Sukarnoputri in 1999. In Thailand, a democratic process has been used to oust the Democrat Party, which supported international-style reforms, in favor of the Thai Rak Thai party that places more emphasis on popularism. In the Philippines, democratically elected President Joseph Estrada was pilloried for incompetence and corruption, before being removed by a demonstration of "people power."

Some ASEAN member states, like the Philippines, Thailand, Cambodia, and Indonesia, have come increasingly to champion democratic norms, notwithstanding such difficulties as corruption and weak parties. It should be noted, however, that these areas of weakness are a by-product of those countries' long and oppressive authoritarian regimes. Other ASEAN members like Vietnam and Laos remain socialist, while still others are nondemocratic in other ways: Brunei is a monarchy and Myanmar remains under military rule. Between these extremes are Malaysia and Singapore that, ranked partly free by some NGOs, have a voting system and limited freedom.

Given these intra-ASEAN differences, it may well be necessary to reinforce the acceptance of diversity as a basis of cooperation. While states should not need to be identical in order to coexist and cooperate in many fields, there is a growing tendency for states to know and care more about what their neighbors do. Thus, were public opinion in a relatively more democratic ASEAN member state to change and hold a neighbor in a more negative light, it could be expected that pressure might be brought to bear on the member state's foreign policy.

The tensions in Thai-Myanmar relations can, in part at least, be explained by such a trend. Similarly, relations between Indonesia and Singapore, as well as between Indonesia and Malaysia, have experienced greater strain since the end of the Suharto regime and the vibrant though sometimes chaotic beginnings of democracy. The government in Indonesia today is more susceptible to shifts in opinion in sectors that influence bilateral relations. Thus, for example, when Malaysia repatriated Indonesian workers in 2002, the negative sentiment among ordinary Indonesians had a severe impact on bilateral ties.

A second factor that shapes attitudes in ASEAN member states is the degree to which a state feels interdependent with other states. Mention has already been made of a number of nontraditional, transboundary sources of insecurity and instability in interstate relations that have impacted ASEAN member states, including the growing incidence of piracy, disputes over fishing grounds, the growing and illegal trade in people, drugs, weapons, and other contraband, as well as environmental disasters, and marine pollution.

Where an ASEAN member state suffers strong negative impacts from these transboundary phenomena, it is more likely to seek to criticize or interfere with the policies of its neighbors. Again, using the example of Thailand and Myanmar, tension between these neighbors relates to the interplay of cross-border issues, including the illegal trade in drugs, women, weapons, and logs. In some cases, Thailand feels aggrieved; in other situations, as with the alleged inflow of weapons to rebel groups, the regime in Myanmar feels that it is adversely affected.

Conversely, countries like Singapore, Malaysia, and Thailand that are relatively more dependent on the regional economy may be anxious to strengthen cooperation in economic and related spheres. They may then press for policy changes in some countries that stand in the way of increased cooperation. More isolated economies may, however, see this as interference in their internal affairs, particularly since trade liberalization and economic integration are no longer limited to external dealings, but affect the internal structures of a country's markets, industries, and administration.

A third factor that helps shape a state's views on sovereignty and intervention is the ability of that state to protect itself against intervention by another state, including its neighbors, Washington, and its allies. While ASEAN comprises small to medium-sized powers, there are notable differences among them. Indonesia, for example, is the world's fourth most populous and largest Muslim country. It is of geopolitical importance and has considerable weight in the international community, notwithstanding its recent difficulties and uncertainties. In many ways, the experience of East Timor was a shock to Indonesia because its standing had, for so long, inured it against complaints and international pressure on the issue of independence for Timor. In contrast, the truly small states in ASEAN, such as Brunei, Cambodia, Laos, and Singapore, may feel that they are more likely to be subject to pressure and intervention.

Beyond size, the ability to fend off unwanted international or regional interference can be linked to diplomatic efforts as well as military preparedness. On this point, Thailand, which is known for its diplomatic adroitness and has never been colonized, may take a different view from others, such as Vietnam, which has a long history of struggle against the big powers. In a different way, the relative military strength and wealth of Singapore may predispose it differently from small states that lack such attributes.

The relationships of ASEAN member states with the United States also differ. The Philippines, for example, is a U.S. ally and has felt comfortable requesting and accepting U.S. military advisers to address conflicts in the Muslim south of the country. In contrast, countries like Malaysia and Indonesia would not, under almost any circumstances, seek a U.S. military presence on their territory. Indeed, some in these countries have expressed concern about the possibility of a longer and greater U.S. presence in the region.

Looking at the ASEAN member states through the prism of these three factors reveals the diversity of dispositions in the association. There is no member state that feels fully safe from intervention, not even Indonesia or Vietnam, the largest member states. Their lower levels of economic development may, in fact, open them more to outside influence and interference from other countries, whether within ASEAN or outside the region. In Indonesia's case, its concern has increased since the financial crisis and developments in East Timor. Thus, with no member state entirely secure and no one state prone to regularly interfere or intervene in the affairs of a neighboring state, ASEAN remains free of regional hegemony.

This does not mean, however, that all ASEAN member states at all times stay clear of what their neighbors might consider interference. Reactions tend to be on a case-by-case basis, with resulting inconsistencies in the practices of almost all countries. Indonesians, for example, may thus resent criticism by groups in the region of the perceived violations of human rights suffered by ethnic Chinese in Jakarta during 1998. However, this has not prevented a significant number of Indonesians from protesting against Malaysia's rounding up and expelling of Indonesian workers in 2002. Similarly, Singapore may resent such incidents of questioning by Manila and protests over the alleged mistreatment of foreign domestic workers as surrounded the Flor Contemplacion episode in the mid-1990s. However, many Singaporeans do express anguish and frustration at the lack of effective Indonesian action to stamp out the fires in its territory that cause smoke haze pollution in Singapore and other countries.

The diversity of ASEAN member states is an inescapable factor in looking at their interdependence and the different situations in which a balance needs to be found between state sovereignty and a choice of cooperation or interference. At best, ASEAN member states seem to be relatively unified in resisting imposition, coercion, and, especially, the use of force, particularly when these are undertaken by non-ASEAN powers.

THE EVOLUTION OF NORMS

Sentiment about sovereignty and intervention relates to a wider view, held by many in ASEAN, on how rules and norms evolve in the international community. The traditional view is that the international system is an anarchy of sovereigns (Bull 1977). In such a system, the consent of a state, either express or implied, is central to the evolution of rules and norms that will bind it. ASEAN member states largely are comforted by such a view of the world. As smaller to medium-sized states, their recurring concern is that larger and more powerful states may shape and mold international norms and relations to suit their own purposes. Thus, when some advocate new norms, like human rights and humanitarian intervention, there are those in ASEAN who tend to be skeptical, in the belief that all such norms are the products of great-power preferences and so should be resisted.

The international system today remains prone to influence from some powerful countries, particularly the United States. Great powers can shape history while smaller states can, at best, hope only to survive it.

Yet, the attitude of smaller and medium-sized states, like those in ASEAN, should not be wholly negative or fatalistic. The push-and-pull evolution of international norms must be accepted and can be influenced even by the smaller states. The international system for making laws and norms is diffuse, incomplete and, more often than not, a matter of establishing principles rather than details. In this context, it is often the case that the international system will declare its acceptance of different principles that can and do clash. The debate about sovereignty and human rights is an example of this. Both are upheld by the international system, even when governments, as the representatives of states, prefer to emphasize the former.

On the specific issue of humanitarian intervention, the norms seem to be in flux. The standard view is that the use of force, other than for self-defense and without the authorization of the United Nations, is illegal. Therefore, many scholars, even in the West, acknowledge that the NATO action in bombing Kosovo was prima facie illegal. However, it is noteworthy that the attempt to pass a resolution condemning NATO intervention also failed. In this regard, the question of humanitarian intervention remains unresolved, both in practice and as a matter of international law and policy.

In this context, the views of ASEAN concerning humanitarian intervention and the associated concepts of sovereignty, human rights, and the use of force, face a fork in the road. Along one path, ASEAN member states may reluctantly consider the issues and confine themselves to shock, protests, or acceptance should the United States and its allies again use coercion or force against a state. This is a defensive or passive stance.

The alternative way forward is for ASEAN member states to more proactively take a fresh look at the norms and their own policies and practices in the conduct of foreign relations as it affects relations among ASEAN member states and with external powers.

In so doing, some tenets may be reaffirmed, such as the aversion to the use of force, while other norms may be revisited and recast. State sovereignty, however, while remaining central, can no longer be seen as absolute while disregarding just domestic state governance and the protection of key human rights. New policies may be initiated as alternatives, designed to enhance cooperation, minimize friction, and provide the peaceful and diplomatic means to head off or limit conflict.

If ASEAN can establish regional peace and order as a security community within its own terms, this example would assist in moving the debate on alternatives to forceful intervention. These means might include the exercise of preventive diplomacy, as promised for the second stage in the ASEAN Regional Forum (ARF), and efforts to train and prepare ASEAN peacekeeping resources to help UN missions. Mechanisms to deal with human-rights violations would be another step to diffuse interstate tension and avoid the possibility of foreign intervention. A concerted ASEAN effort to join in the debate on humanitarian intervention might also influence international opinion and ASEAN's policies on the issues raised.

The world and the ASEAN region today are too interdependent to hold to an absolute dogma of state sovereignty. Thus, if the unilateral imposition or use of force by a foreign power or powers is to be avoided, ASEAN member states—individually and collectively—should aim to deal with each other, external powers, and their own citizens in ways that enhance peace and cooperation and avoid the transgressions that can trigger international concern and intervention.

NOTES

1. For an analysis of the ASEAN way, see Antolik (1990) and Haas (1989). For a view on noninterference and the interplay between preventive diplomacy and measures short of the use of force, see Tay (1999a). Also see Ramcharan (2000).

2. "The nations of Asia view one another as strategic rivals even as they cooperate on economic matters. Wars between them are not likely, but neither are they excluded. The international order of Asia therefore resembles that of nineteenth-century Europe more than that of the twenty-first-century North Atlantic" (Kissinger 2002, 110).

3. According to international law, an act carried out with the consent of a state cannot be interpreted as intervention. However, there may be instances in which consent is given under such a degree of pressure or is so manufactured that the legality and legitimacy of the act is held in doubt. Bearing in mind the scope and length of this chapter, however, the authors have been able to do no more than refer to the widespread resentment in Indonesia concerning events in East Timor, without discussing the details.

4. In 2000 and 2002, the ASEAN Institutes for Strategic and International Studies (ASEAN-ISIS) convened two civil society groups, comprising nongovernmental and other organizations. Each assembly comprised more than 300 representatives who were involved in networks dealing with environment, human rights, agriculture, urban poverty, development assistance, and the media.

5. Under Article 2 (4) of the Charter of the United Nations, the use of force is prohibited. Exceptions are made only for self-defense (Article 51), and when its use is authorized by the United Nations (Article 42). But this has not always been the case. Previously, tradition had it that so-called just and

holy wars were allowed, and that only unjust wars were illegitimate. War was perceived to be legitimate if tied to a religious or moral cause. Hugo Grotius (1583–1645) argued that good grounds for war included defense, indemnity, and punishment. As the state shed its religious and moral origins, however, the notion of a just war faded and war became a legitimate tool of state craft. In realpolitik and for positivists, there remained only procedural questions, such as whether there had been a formal declaration of war. Even in the early twentieth century, the use of force was not illegal, and the League of Nations (1920–1946) considered war to be an international concern that was to be regulated (Articles 10, 11, 12, and 16), for which reason formal procedures, such as the three-month cooling-off period, were instituted. Even after World War I, following the 1928 Pact of Paris (Kellogg-Briand Pact), despite the fact that war was generally renounced, lesser forms of force were not prohibited.

6. Authorization by the UN General Assembly under the "Uniting for Peace" Resolution (1950) is another possibility, given the historical perception that the UN General Assembly enjoys a secondary responsibility for keeping the international peace. This mechanism has been used before (on the Korean peninsula, in the Congo crisis), but has fallen into disuse.

7. There is a nongovernmental working group for the establishment of an ASEAN human rights mechanism, to which one of the authors of this chapter belongs. However, the efforts of the group have not been successful to date.

BIBLIOGRAPHY

Antolik, Michael. 1990. *ASEAN and the Diplomacy of Accommodation.* Armonk, N.Y.: M.E. Sharpe.

Anwar Ibrahim. 1997. "Crisis Prevention." *Newsweek* (21 July).

Brooks, Stephen G., and William C. Wohlforth. 2002. "American Primacy in Perspective." *Foreign Affairs* 81(4): 20–33.

Bull, Hedley. 1977. *The Anarchical Society: A Study of Order in World Politics.* London: Macmillan.

Haas, Michael. 1989. *The Asian Way to Peace: A Story of Regional Cooperation.* Westport, Conn.: Praeger.

Kissinger, Henry. 2002. In *Does America Need a Foreign Policy?: Toward a Diplomacy for the 21st Century.* Carmichael, Calif.: Touchstone Books.

"Present at the creation: A survey of America's world role." 2002. *The Economist* (29 June–5 July).

Rajaretnam, M. 1999. "Principles in Crisis: The Need for New Directions." In Kao Kim Hourn and Jeffrey A. Kaplan, eds. *Principles Under Pressure:*

Cambodia and ASEAN's Non-Interference Policy. Phnom Penh: Cambodian Institute for Cooperation and Peace.

Ramcharan, Robin. 2000. "ASEAN and Non-Interference: A Principle Maintained." *Contemporary Southeast Asia* 22(1).

Sukma, Rizal. 1997. "ASEAN dan problematik iintervensi konstruktif" (ASEAN and the problematique of constructive intervention). *Kompas* (July).

———. 2000. "Indonesia and Non-Intervention Debate in Southeast Asia." In David Dickens and Guy Wilson-Roberts, eds. *Non-Intervention and State Sovereignty in the Asia-Pacific*. Wellington, N.Z.: Centre for Strategic Studies.

Tan, Iris, and Simon Tay. 2002. *Preventing Future Fires: Special Report on the Indonesian Fires and Haze*. Singapore: Singapore Institute of International Affairs.

Tay, Simon S. C. 1996. "Human Rights and Culture: The Singapore Example." McGill Law Journal 41(4).

———. 1999a. "Preventive Diplomacy in the ASEAN Regional Forum: Principles and Possibilities." In Desmond Ball and Amitav Acharya, eds. *The Next Stage: Preventive Diplomacy and Security Co-operation in the Asia Pacific Region*. Canberra Papers in Strategy and Defense, Strategic and Defense Studies Centre, Australian National University, and Institute of Defense and Strategic Studies, Nanyang Technological University.

———. 1999b. "Southeast Asian Fires: The Challenge to International Law and Development." *Georgetown International Environmental Law Review* (Winter).

———. 2001. "ASEAN Institutions and Processes." In Simon S. C. Tay, Jesus P. Estanislao, and Hadi Soesastro, eds. *Reinventing ASEAN*. Singapore: Institute of Southeast Asian Studies.

———. 2002. "America at War: A View from the Periphery." A report on observations during an Eisenhower fellowship.

Tay, Simon S. C., Jesus P. Estanislao, and Hadi Soesastro, eds. *Reinventing ASEAN*. Singapore: Institute of Southeast Asian Studies.

About the Contributors

WATANABE KŌJI is executive advisor to the Japan Federation of Economic Organizations (Keidanren) and senior fellow at the Japan Center for International Exchange. He was Japanese ambassador to Russia from 1993 to 1996 and ambassador to Italy from 1992 to 1993. He was also deputy minister for foreign affairs, sherpa for the G-7 Houston and London summits of 1990 and 1991, and Japanese cochairman of the U.S.-Japan Structural Impediments Initiative Talks. Ambassador Watanabe joined the Ministry of Foreign Affairs upon graduating from the University of Tokyo in 1956 and served as director-general of the Information Analysis, Research and Planning Bureau and director-general of the Economic Affairs Bureau. He was a visiting fellow at the Woodrow Wilson School of Princeton University (1957–1958) and at the Center for International Affairs of Harvard University (1973–1974). His other overseas posts include counsellor at the Japanese Embassy in Saigon (1974–1976), minister at the Japanese Embassy in Beijing (1981–1984), and ambassador to Saudi Arabia (1988–1989).

JIA QINGGUO is professor and associate dean of the School of International Studies of Peking University. Dr. Jia has taught at the University of Vermont, Cornell University, the University of California at San Diego, the University of Sydney, and Peking University. He has published extensively on U.S.-China relations, Sino-Taiwan relations,

Chinese foreign policy, and Chinese politics. He is a member of the Editorial Boards of the *Journal of Contemporary China* (USA), *Political Science* (New Zealand), *International Relations of the Asia-Pacific* (Japan), and *China Review* (Hong Kong). He is also vice president of the China Association for Asia-Pacific Studies, board member of the China Association of American Studies, and board member of the National Taiwan Studies Association. He received his Ph.D. from Cornell University in 1988 and was a Research Fellow at the Brookings Institution in 1985–1986.

KIM SUNG-HAN is an associate professor in the Department of American Studies at the Institute of Foreign Affairs and National Security (IFANS), Ministry of Foreign Affairs & Trade in Seoul, Korea. Dr. Kim also teaches at Korea University, advises Korea's National Security Council (NSC), and works as a guest columnist for the *Korea Herald*. Before joining IFANS in 1994, he served as research fellow at the Institute of Social Sciences and as an expert advisor to the Prime Minister's Committee for Globalization. A specialist in U.S. foreign policy and international security, Dr. Kim has published widely in his field. His recent publications include "End of Humanitarian Intervention?" in *Orbis* (Fall 2003); "U.S. Policy toward the Korean Peninsula & ROK-U.S. Security Cooperation," in *Korea and World Affairs* (Spring 2001); and "Human Security and Regional Cooperation: Preparing for the Twenty-first Century," in *Asia's Emerging Regional Order* (2000). Dr. Kim received his Ph.D. from the University of Texas at Austin.

MURATA KŌJI is associate professor of Diplomatic History in the Department of Political Science at Doshisha University in Kyoto. Prior to assuming this position, he was associate professor of American Studies at the School of Integrated Arts and Sciences at Hiroshima. Professor Murata received his M.A. in international relations and his Ph.D. in political science from Kobe University. He also obtained his M.Phil. in political science from George Washington University, where he studied as a Fulbright scholar. Dr. Murata's specialties include the history of the U.S.-Japan security relationship, American alliance policy toward Northeast Asia, and Japan's defense policy. He received the Yomiuri Merit Award for Young Opinion Leadership in 1996, the Shimizu Hiroshi Award from the Japan Association for American Studies, the Suntory Academic Prize in 1999, and the Yoshida Shigeru Award in 2000. Professor Murata has authored two books, *President Carter's Policy for U.S. Troop Withdrawal from South Korea* (1998) and *The First U.S. Defense Secretary James Forrestal* (1999), and many articles in Japanese and English.

Air Commodore JASJIT SINGH is former director of the Institute for Defence Studies and Analyses (1987–2001), as well as the former director of operations of the Indian Air Force. He is a member of the National Security Advisory Board and consultant to the Standing Committee of Defence of the Parliament. Dr. Singh is author or editor of more than two dozen books on strategic and security issues, including *Non-provocative Defence* (1989), *Nuclear India* (1998), *Kargil 1999: Pakistan's Fourth War for Kashmir* (1999), and *India's Defence Spending* (2000). Dr. Singh was a member of the International Commission for a New Asia and the International Commission for Peace and Food. He has received national awards from the president of India, including an AVSM (Ati Vasisht Seva Medal) for sustained distinguished service of an exceptional order, a Vr C (Vir Chakra) for gallantry in the face of an enemy (awarded for operational missions during the 1971 war), and a VM (Vayu Sena Medal) for a distinguished act of gallantry and service of special significance to the Indian Air Force.

RIZAL SUKMA is director of studies at the Centre for Strategic and International Studies (CSIS), Jakarta. Dr. Sukma is also the secretary to the International Relations Bureau of the Central Executive Board of Muhammadiyah (the second-largest Islamic organization in Indonesia) and visiting lecturer at the Post-Graduate Faculty of the University of Indonesia. He has worked extensively on Southeast Asian security issues, the Association of Southeast Asian Nations, Indonesia's foreign policy, and domestic political changes in Indonesia. He recently contributed chapters on a variety of issues—such as human security and security issues in Indonesia—to several publications, including *The Quest for Human Security: The Next Phase of ASEAN?* (2001), *Non-Traditional Security Issues in Southeast Asia* (2001), *Asia Pacific Security Outlook 2001* (2001), *Memory and History in East and Southeast Asia: Issues of Identity in International Relations* (2001), and *Non-Intervention and State Sovereignty in the Asia-Pacific* (2000). Dr. Sukma most recently authored the publication *Indonesia and China: The Politics of A Troubled Relation-ship* (1999). Dr. Sukma received his Ph.D. in International Relations from the London School of Economics (LSE) in 1997.

SIMON S. C. TAY is associate professor at the Faculty of Law, National University of Singapore. He concurrently serves as chairman of the Singapore Institute of International Affairs, a member of the ASEAN Institutes for Strategic and International Studies, and as chairman of the National Environment Agency, a major government body in Singapore. In autumn 2003, he was visiting professor at Harvard Law School and at the Fletcher School of Harvard University. He was a non-elected member of Parliament (1997–2001), and is one of two Singaporean representatives on the ASEAN Regional Forum Register of Eminent Persons and Experts, while he also serves on a number of international panels including those for the United Nations Environment Programme, the Asia Society, and the Asia Pacific Forum on Environment and Development. Professor Tay received his LL.M. from Harvard University Law School and LL.B. from the National University of Singapore. His numerous publications include *The Enemy Within: Combating Corruption in Asia* (2003), *Reinventing ASEAN in Crisis and Change* (2001), *The South East Asian Fires: The Challenge to International Environmental Law* (1999), and *The ASEAN Regional Forum and Preventive Diplomacy* (1998).

Index

Japan Center for
International Exchange

Founded in 1970, the Japan Center for International Exchange (JCIE) is an independent, nonprofit, and nonpartisan organization dedicated to strengthening Japan's role in international affairs. JCIE believes that Japan faces a major challenge in augmenting its positive contributions to the international community, in keeping with its position as one of the world's largest industrial democracies.Operating in a country where policymaking has traditionally been dominated by the government bureaucracy, JCIE has played an important role in broadening debate on Japan's international responsibilities by conducting international and cross-sectional programs of exchange, research, and discussion.

JCIE creates opportunities for informed policy discussions; it does not take policy positions. JCIE programs are carried out with the collaboration and cosponsorship of many organizations. The contacts developed through these working relationships are crucial to JCIE's efforts to increase the number of Japanese from the private sector engaged in meaningful policy research and dialogue with overseas counterparts. JCIE receives no government subsidies; rather, funding comes from private foundation grants, corporate contributions, and contracts.